Trashed or Treasured?

A Short, Practical Theology of Aging

(UPDATED & REVISED)

Trashed or Treasured?

A Short, Practical Theology of Aging

(UPDATED & REVISED)

Glenn Bryant Havumaki, D. Min.

ARPress
ILLUMINATING IDEAS
EMPOWERING VOICES

Trashed or Treasured?
A Short, Practical Theology of Aging
©2012 Glenn Bryant Havumaki. 2nd Printing 2023

Unless otherwise indicated, Bible quotations are taken from The New King James Version of the Bible. Copyright © 1982 by Thomas Nelson.

Scriptures marked NIV are taken from the HOLY BIBLE, NEW INTERNATIONAL VERSION,. Copyright © 1973, 1978, 1984 by International Bible Society. Used by permission of Zondervan Publishing House. All rights reserved.

Scriptures marked KJV are taken from The Holy Bible, King James Version. Copyright © 1972 by Thomas Nelson Inc., Camden, New Jersey 08103.

Scriptures marked NASV are taken from the NEW AMERICAN STANDARD BIBLE®, Copyright © 1960, 1962, 1963, 1971, 1972, 1973, 1975, 1977, 1995 by The Lockman Foundation, LaHabra, CA Used by permission. All rights reserved.

Scriptures marked ESV are taken from The Holy Bible, English Standard Version* (ESV*) copyright © 2001by Crossway Bibles, a publishing ministry of Good News Publishers. Used by permission. All rights reserved.

ARPress
45 Dan Road Suite 5
Canton, MA 02021

Hotline: 1(888) 821-0229
Fax: 1(508) 545-7580

Ordering Information:
Quantity sales. Special discounts are available on quantity purchases by corporations, associations, and others. For details, contact the publisher at the address above.

Printed in the United States of America.

ISBN-13:   Softcover   979-8-89330-402-2
            eBook   979-8-89330-403-9

Library of Congress Control Number: 2024900789

Contents

Endorsements

"I agreed to read this book as a favor to my friend, Glenn. It turned out to be a favor for me. The book is informative, interesting, helpful, and challenging. Above all it is Scriptural. This book can be helpful to those who are advanced in age but it can also be helpful to young people who need help in formulating a meaningful purpose for their lives. It will be especially helpful to Seminary students who are preparing for a life of ministry, to counselors, to busy pastors, and leaders of senior citizen groups.

Points are illustrated by interesting human-interest stories. At the end of every chapter there is a section called, "Reflect and Grow," which asks penetrating questions for the reader to ponder. I benefited much from reading this book. I wish that I could have read it as I was starting out in ministry." **Dr. Stanley R. Allaby, Pastor Emeritus of Black Rock Congregational Church in Fairfield, CT, and Professor Emeritus of Homiletics at the former Bethel Seminary of the East, Auburn, MA**

"Glenn Havumaki writes from experience and with passion. His reflections on the role of the church and older adults should be in every pastor's leadership DNA. The 40/50 Window is the new challenge of the church. Havumaki presents a solid case for equipping and engaging those living in that 'Window' for meaningful ministry; and for serving, *not forgetting our 'veteran saints' as they reach life's final turn."* **Ward Tannenberg, Writer, Pastor retired, PhD Theology**

"Having served with Dr. Havumaki as a co-laborer in senior ministry, this book comes as no surprise to me. In a society that focuses primarily on the younger generation, it's refreshing to see how the Lord can fashion and use an individual for His express purpose. Glenn's unique approach to senior ministry is pragmatic yet profound and very user friendly. As Dr. Havumaki weaves you through the pages of this book, you will inevitably get caught up in his passion to serve and to love as Jesus did. This is a book about life from its genesis to the end of time. The narratives are true; the people are real. This is a book about you and me!" **Rev. William H. Echols, President/Executive Director: Community Chaplain Service, Inc.**

"Only Chaplain Glenn Havumaki, D.Min., could write this book. He has spent his entire adult life ministering with older adults and his words reflect depth of experience, well-honed theology and a contagious passion for ministry. Dr. Havumaki illustrates God's value for long life through the study of Scripture and the journeys of Biblical characters. He also shares the inspirational stories and sage advice of older adults, many which transformed his own life through the years. Finally, Dr. Havumaki provides practical and dynamic ideas for pastors and church leaders as they minister to generations that are "coming of age." We've served with Dr. Havumaki and We've seen how deeply he cares about older adults, their spiritual growth and legacy. I hope and pray that readers will heed his challenge to treasure and not trash those who have lived a long time and now stand on the threshold of eternity." **Richard and Leona Bergstrom Co-Directors, Re-Ignite (www.Re-Ignite. net)**

Dedication

I dedicate this book to the Lord in gratefulness for the spiritual gifts and natural abilities that he wove into my life; and for the experiences that He allowed me to have so that I could put into print those things that I hope will multiply, through others, my passion for the souls of adults over age fifty. I would also dedicate this book to the two ministries that have allowed me to learn, to serve, and to grow in the knowledge of ministry to, through and with older adults: The Community Chaplain Service, Inc and the Elim Park Baptist Home. Together, they gave me a total of thirty-eight years of ministry experience. May God continue to bless and use these ministries to encourage, care for and bring many to a safe passage across the bridge of eternal significance; heaven bound and secure in the saving knowledge of Jesus Christ.

Acknowledgments

I am…Grateful to my wife Sandy for her patience over the years as I have poured hours into ministry and then writing about this passion that God has given me to motivate older adults to grow in the knowledge of Jesus Christ, the Word of God, and to serve Him until the very last breath. She has also assisted much with edits through the years.

Grateful to God and those encouragers He put into my life as I was thinking this manuscript through: the group of senior adult leaders who sat through my first presentation of a theology on aging and encouraged me to write a book; the young pastor who listened to my teaching at a community prayer day service and said, "your teaching taught me things today that I have never really thought about" and invited me to share it with his under age thirty congregation. He said that even though a young church they all had parents and grandparents and needed to hear this. I am also grateful to a fellow servant in ministry, Paul, who took the time to read my thoughts and encouraged me as partner in ministry. To those who were willing to assist by reading the manuscript in later stages and offered helpful comments and critique: especially Douglas Fombelle, at the time of my original publication, Dean of Bethel Seminary of the East and others whose endorsements are recorded in this book. God continually put people in my path that gave encouragement to write.

Grateful for Mrs. Kuhrt and Mrs. Forbes who allowed me to use the meaningful stories of their husband's love and service for God.

Grateful for my son, Erik and daughter-in-law, Kayla, who accepted the challenge to get the final manuscript ready for submission.

Grateful to the staff of the first publisher, especially Michael Caryl, Publishing Consultant and Karla Castellon who offered much encouragement to a new author and now in this new edition, Chloe Bennett, Senior Author Advisor, and Phoebe Hamilton, Fulfillment Officer.

Extremely grateful for Dr. Larry Keefauver and his staff who edited the book and offered such helpful suggestions for the final presentation of the manuscript and getting me through the rough spots in this book. I add my grateful appreciation to our friend, Joyce Crandley, for editing this latest edition of the book.

I am likely to overlook someone in this listing and if so, God knows how grateful I have been to all who have encouraged me with the result of writing my first book. Praise God!

About The Author

My ministry to older adults began in 1976 when I left a pastorate to go into a newly founded ministry. The vision of its founder, Reverend David Kimball, was to bring comfort and care, along with the gospel of Jesus Christ, into institutions of all kinds—hospitals, nursing homes, prisons, senior housing and even industry. The purpose of this community-based ministry called the Community Chaplain Service, Inc. was to enlist volunteers from local churches and to train and build a volunteer team to minister in these institutions. Most of the ministry, at the time, was targeted toward nursing homes. It seems that I came full-circle and served on the Board of Directors as Chairman, until my resignation in 2015, to become part of the Christian Grandparenting Network as a Certified Ministry Partner now a presenter of the Courageous Grandparenting Seminar.

Soon after beginning with this ministry, I became the Protestant chaplain in four nursing homes and recruited and developed a team of about twenty volunteers who served in a total of seven nursing homes. It was in this experience that the Lord began to burden me for older adult ministry. I found that I was comfortable with older persons. The Lord had blessed me with a personality and giftedness that benefited such a ministry, along with a voice that was clear and readily heard by most of the people to whom I ministered.

In August of 1978, my parents visited a family member at a retirement community in Connecticut, and on that day the Chaplain resigned. Being concerned about our financial situation in a *faith ministry* and the fact that we had recently given birth to our first child, my mother called and suggested that I inquire about this position that was now open. I was content and challenged in my present ministry; but after much prodding from my mother, I made the contact and received a packet of information. I read through the job description and other materials; then promptly threw it all on a shelf in my office and thought—maybe someday in the future.

Little did I know that through many ups and downs, I would eventually accept the call ten months later to become the second full-time Chaplain and Director of Christian Ministries of the Elim Park Baptist Home, Inc. in Cheshire, Connecticut. I completed almost thirty-five years of ministry, and can still honestly say, "This was one of God's big surprises in my life." Though I had an interest in the chaplaincy, I never thought that it would be in a retirement community and certainly would never have guessed that it would be such a long-term position. To this day, residents, family members, staff, administration and board members constantly affirm my ministry. I continue to feel blessed in that I can honestly say I did not have one day when I was ready to quit and move on to something else, which also affirmed my calling and the blessing of God.

For more than twenty-five years I was involved in a ministry of our denomination called Converge Second Half for Him (formerly BGC Gold). [1] This was a ministry to adults over the age of fifty, and in the local region I served as Coordinator. On the national level I was active on a National Leadership Team and had the privilege of serving on a "think tank" team of six, assigned the task to design and initiate a training module to prepare the denomination churches for greater effectiveness in older adult ministries. It was as a part of this responsibility that I was asked to prepare a presentation on the *Theology of Aging* which developed into this book.

In March of 2004, I completed requirements for a Doctor of Ministry Degree and wrote a thesis on ***Faith Development of Older Adults Living in a Continuing Care Retirement Community.*** I recognized the ministry of Elim Park as an extension of the local church, and therefore was involved in writing articles, leading workshops, and trying to find avenues to challenge the church and its leaders—especially the evangelical church—to a deeper involvement with adults fifty years and older in their congregations and in their communities. Since 1984 I still participate on a local Christian radio station program called Bread of Life Devotions, sharing a week of devotions during National Nursing Home Week, to remind families and the church to not forget "homebound" and nursing home residents so that they do not experience separation anxiety and a lack of spiritual care.

I hope that this book challenges the reader to find a biblical basis for ministry that will prepare people to live out their older adult years purposefully. Older adults need to be prepared to cross over *the bridge of eternal significance* with the confidence that eternal life will be theirs as they enter into the presence of God with Jesus Christ.

Preface

Trashed or Treasured?

That which is old is either trashed or treasured! Thrown out if it is junk; treasured if it has value. If it is considered an antique we hold on to it, display it and get good money for it; *and the older the better.*

Let me illustrate. Several years ago my family cleaned out my grandmother's home after her death. My wife had brought home an old bedspread and a throw/cover for a couch. Not because she wanted it, but because we had an antique dealer in our town that purchased old clothe, clothes, etc. Her words on many occasions were, "Never throw anything away! Let us who know things of value take a look first." My wife had the cloth in the garage and decided that rather than bringing it to the antique dealer we should bring it to the dump, saying, "No one will want *that!*" My daughter came home as my wife and I were having a discussion about this. I wanted to take it to the dealer and she thought it to be worthless. When our daughter heard our conversation, she said, "I'll just take it to Debbie and let *her* decide!" She rescued the cloth and later came back with $125.00. You see, there was great value in what my wife considered too old and would have thrown out; yet had great value!

The title for this book was birthed out of the above family experience. We live in a culture that wants to throw out that which is old: not only things, but people, too. In the pages of this book I want you to look at human beings from God's perspective and I am going to challenge you with what I believe the Scriptures seem to say about honoring God and the older adult. It will be a three-step approach: Respected, Rejected and Reconnected.

We need to explore the Scriptures because there is a compelling biblical and theological basis for the church to minister to maturing adults over the age of fifty. I believe that we must purpose to include this population in our planning for ministry, and more so as this fifty plus population comes upon us as a fast moving wave; more like a tsunami!

There are other books about ministering to older adults that do contain some theological basis for ministry; and at least one that presents an excellent theology on aging from an evangelical viewpoint, but rather lengthy. My purpose is to put this short, practical theology on aging into the hands of the family, seminary student, counselor, busy pastor, or leader of the older adult ministry in the local church, and to challenge adults to find purpose in their older years. It can be read in a brief time to help give a biblical basis and perspective for ministry with this growing segment of our population.

We can no longer ignore this group for statistics tell us that an adult turns fifty years old every seven seconds in the United States. This group of seventy-eight million boomers began to turn sixty-five years old in 2011 and will continue until 2029, when most statisticians tell us that one out of every five Americans will be over the age of sixty-five. According to the latest census figures it is estimated that the fastest growing segment of the US population are those over the age of 85

It is also noteworthy that another 1.8 million older adults live in the nursing homes of America, and each year two-thirds of them die and are replaced as quickly as they can clean the rooms. Unless the church sees this as a viable mission field, many will go on to a Christ-less eternity! In mission terminology this is "a hidden people in plain view" of every church in America with many residents who would welcome the message of the gospel. [2]

Introduction

Finishing Well

Early in my ministry as the Chaplain of a retirement community, one of the resident men spoke at an orientation for new residents of the "home." He told a story that made a deep and memorable impression upon my heart. It had a message that spoke clearly of the purpose of life for the older Christian. It continues to remind me of the goal—the lasting purpose of a maturing faith as I minister to, through and with older adults. The story goes like this. A little girl took out her box of crayons and a piece of paper and climbed up onto a chair at the kitchen table. She began to draw a picture. After a little while her mother came into the kitchen and as she walked by the table she looked over the girl's shoulder at the picture. Not able to recognize anything on the paper, she asked, "What are you drawing, honey?" The girl looked up at her Mom and proudly announced, "I'm drawing a picture of God!" Her Mom thought for a minute and then said, as gently as she could, "But honey, nobody knows what God looks like." To that the little girl drew back her shoulders, took a deep breath, looked at her Mom, and said, with a note of pride, "Well, they will when I am finished!"

The actions of our lives are creating a picture that reveals who we are in the eyes of others. For adults in the second half of life the story invites several questions.

- *Is the picture that I am drawing with my life giving others a better picture of God?*
- *When my life reaches its end how will my family, friends, or acquaintances remember me?*
- *Will they have a better picture of what God looks like because of my life and my God-like character?*
- *Will they see a strong-lined picture of a maturing faith that was being evidenced more and more throughout the years?*
- *Will they only see the struggles, the trials or maybe even a dementia of some sort?*
- *Will the picture of my life be that of fading lines of a weak faith; one that did not give evidence of a growing and strong faith?*

These are some sobering questions!

The Apostle Paul's final lines on the picture of his life are drawn in the words of 2 Timothy 4:6-7, when he writes, "For I am already being poured out as a drink offering, and the time of my departure is at hand. I have fought the good fight, *I have finished the race, and I have kept the faith.*" (Italics mine) *Finishing well* should be the goal of each Christian older adult.

Warren Wiersbe includes in the "Song of the Mid-Life Crisis" a quote of F.B. Meyer, in which he said to a friend, "I do hope my Father will let the river of my life go flowing fully until the finish." Then the saintly British preacher added, "I don't want it to end in a swamp."[3]

Finishing well is a godly goal! This is the intent of the Scriptures and exemplified by Jesus Christ as He came to the end of his earthly life, and said, "I have glorified You on the earth. *I have finished the work* which You have given Me to do." (John 17:4, Italics added by author.)

Chapter One

The Beginning of the Finish

Finish well! If we are going to *finish well* we have to remember where we started. We must zoom in on the beginning of God's relationship and purpose for mankind. It began in the Garden and goes all the way to the grave. We read of man's beginning in Genesis, (sometimes called the book of beginnings) "Then God said, 'Let Us make man in Our image, according to Our likeness….'" So God created man in His *own* image; in the image of God He created him; male and female He created them." (Genesis 1:26–27) The *how* of man's creation is better explained in the next chapter: "And the LORD God formed man of the dust of the ground, and breathed into his nostrils the breath of life; and man became a living being" (2:7). God created each person in His image, uniquely breathed into him His own life (causing each one to have a God awareness and an eternal soul), and then instructed him and provided for him. He gave them a home. "The LORD God planted a garden eastward in Eden, and there He put the man whom He had formed" (2:8); a job and a purpose, "Then God blessed them, and God said to them, "Be fruitful and multiply; fill the earth and subdue it; have dominion over the fish of the sea, over the birds of the air, and over every living thing that moves on the earth" (1:28). God also began the family when Adam felt incomplete as he did his work for God.

"So Adam gave names to all cattle, to the birds of the air, and to every beast of the field. But for Adam there was not found a helper comparable to him" (2:20). God responded and answered his need. "And the LORD God caused a deep sleep to fall on Adam, and he slept; and He took one of his ribs, and closed up the flesh in its place. Then the rib which the LORD God had taken from man He made into a woman, and He brought her to the man. And Adam said: "This is now bone of my bones and flesh of my flesh; she shall be called Woman, because she was taken out of Man" (2:21-23).

More Than Relationship

When God created the heavens and the earth and all that was in it, excluding mankind, He said, "It is good." But when God created mankind in His image–it brought an exhilarating response from God: "It is *very* good." Man is in a special category of creation, because God breathed into his nostrils life and man became a living being" (2:8). Human beings were designed to have a special relationship with God; an honored relationship. They were created not only to have this unique relationship, but as a result, to have responsibility and purpose in the world in which they lived. They were created not only in God's image, but also in His likeness.

Men and women were created with emotions, creativity, an ability to commune with God, and a body that was planned by God from eternity—the same type of body that He himself would have one day (Galatians 4:4). Jesus was born to die (Hebrews 10:5-10)! Man's life could have been eternal, with no death, had he not sinned. In the garden God said to Adam, "Of every tree of the garden you may freely eat; but of the tree of the knowledge of good and evil you shall not eat, for in the day that you eat of it you shall surely die." (2:16-17)

This meant spiritual as well as physical death: a separation from God and separation from his fellow man. Sin also brought into the world all the things that contribute to the aging process and eventually lead to death: hard work, sweat (of the brow), sickness, sorrow, sadness, excruciating pain in childbirth, etc. God said in Genesis 3:19, "In the sweat of your face you shall eat bread till you return to the ground, for out of it you were taken; for dust you *are*, and to dust you shall return." Man was created out of the dust of the earth at the command of God and would also return to the dust of the earth at the command of God—at death (cf. Hebrews 9:27). Therefore the term, "dust to dust" is heard most often in the final tributes to one's life at a cemetery. The Psalmist reminds us, "For He knows our frame; he remembers that we *are* dust" (Psalm 103:14). In other words, God knew the weaknesses of mankind brought about by the first sin, but with this problem came the solution: the promise of the Savior; who became for mankind the means of salvation.

> No matter how healthy we are or how long we live and even with all the research, medical advances, and available wellness programs to increase our lifespan to one hundred years or more; dust and the grave awaits us unless the Lord returns to take His loved ones home earlier.

He knows our frame and how long it will last. He promises to provide all that we need to keep this temporary house in tact until His call to return to *dust*. The Psalmist also reminds us that only God knows the number of the days that each of us will live upon this earth. His Word says, "In Thy book they were all written, the days that were ordained for me, when as yet there was not one of them" (Psalm 139:16, NASV).

What a wonderful reminder! God knows not only the end from the beginning, but every moment in between from conception to death. No matter how healthy we are or how long we live and even with all the research, medical advances, and available wellness programs to increase our lifespan to one hundred years or more; dust and the grave await us unless the Lord returns to take His loved ones home earlier. Physically, we live here on planet Earth only as long as God allows. It is His will, not ours! Psalm 90:10 shares these words, "The days of our lives *are* seventy years; and if by reason of strength *they are* eighty years, yet their boast is only labor and sorrow; for it *is* soon cut off, and we fly away."

When we sincerely turn to God through His Son, Jesus, we are "passed from death to life" (Romans 5:8-10). The sinful and marred image is restored by grace and faith in Jesus Christ. God offers forgiveness of sin, reconciliation and eternal life to mankind by the receiving of His Son. Outside of Jesus, there is no offer of forgiveness—only the prospect of eternal separation from God. When we invite Jesus into our life His spirit makes us eternally alive in Him and the process of restoration begins. The life of the Son, the true image of God, is formed in us and we are promised eternal life with our Creator. He promises that we will be made perfectly like Him (1 Corinthians 15:47-54). When we become a believer through the new birth (John 3:3 – 7), the Creator (Colossians 1:16; John 1:1, 3, 10; Hebrews 1: 1 - 2; Ephesians 3:8-9) of life gives new life and we are "renewed in knowledge after the image of Him that created him" (Colossians 3:10, KJV).

Living Is Preparation for Death!

I want to introduce you to a man named Wesley Kuhrt. **(Note:** *Except for Wesley Kuhrt and Lou Forbes all the other names have*

been changed to protect their identity. The above mentioned men have made a great impression upon my life, and I gained permission from their wives to identify them by name in their stories.) I met Wes when I went to the church he attended one Sunday evening to give a presentation of the ministry at Elim Park. As I went into the church, I saw a man with a mop in his hand cleaning the bathroom and then moving some chairs around. I naturally assumed that he was the janitor. It was not until sometime later that I learned about this man's life.

He was one of the founding members of this church and had a wonderful family. He had served as the Senior Vice-President of Technology for United Technologies, a conglomerate of businesses involved in the production of materials for the defense systems of America. He had also played an active role in Otis Elevator and some other businesses in Connecticut and around the world.

At one time, he had been the President of Sikorsky Aircraft in Stratford, Connecticut and brought it from a business that was many millions of dollars in the red to a successful business status. His father-in-law, who lived at Elim Park told me that United Technologies was naming a building in Florida after Wes. However, due to the fact that he was such a humble man, he did not even tell his family about it! His wife knew, but he did not want the children or anyone else to know. As it turned out, the children were invited and flew down to Florida on the morning of the dedication as a complete surprise to Wes.

He was a man of great ability, position, means–but most of all, a humble man of God whose life touched many for Christ. I would have to say that he was probably one of the most humble men that I have ever met. After he retired from United Technologies, he served on the board of directors for an English company and

traveled to England once a month on the Concord jet. He let me know that he used that travel time to pray for Elim Park and my ministry as Chaplain.

I was blessed by this man's life as he lifted me up in prayer. He died, tragically, as the result of a car accident. Immediately after his death, as the pastor of the church walked out of the hospital room with Wes' sister, Prudence, she said, *"For this day, Wes lived his whole life."* The words were forever etched into my memory.

Mrs. Wesley Kuhrt gave me a copy of a letter that told of the desire of the company to remember and honor Wes after his death. The Chairman and Chief Executive Officer of United Technologies wrote, "As you know, we have been investigating ways to honor Wes for his many years of distinguished service to the Corporation. The options were fairly standard; scholarships, professorships and plaques. However, none of these memorials seemed quite right. To me, and others who knew Wes, the best way to show our respect is to encourage others to follow his example of compassion and caring." The company joined together with the YMCA to establish the Wesley A. Kuhrt Youth Citizenship Award for Community Service, which would honor local area youths, ages fifteen to twenty, who reach out to help others in their community on a regular basis. His wife, Elaine, said, "I thought that it was special for a secular company to want to honor Wes for his compassion and caring!" She went on to say that this program is now in its twenty-second year and they now give four one thousand dollar awards, each year, to the young people that meet the requirements for this distinguished award that honors a man that honored others.

Finishing well! Leaving a legacy! Some time ago I read a statement that went something like this: we need to live lives that are not so much defined by duration, but rather by donation. We need to live life in preparation for the day

> We need to live lives that are not so much defined by duration, but rather donation.

that we die because when we approach life with that attitude we are more apt to improve the quality of our earthly lives. Our lives need to be filled with godly character that reflects Christ and will be honored by the fellowship of believers, the world around us, and most of all by God.

Just Passin' Through

The day after I started a Bible study for staff, a nurse in her mid-fifties came to me and said, "I was awake all night thinking about something you said last night. You said that good works are not enough to guarantee eternal life in heaven. If that is true, how can I know that I can get there?"

I had the opportunity to tell her that it was only through putting our faith in Jesus Christ, His death in our place on the cross, and His overcoming of death through the resurrection that solidifies salvation. Her response was simple, "I want to do that!" She was on her way to a nursing call, so I simply gave her a tract that explained the way of salvation and told her to read it after work sometime and call me with any questions.

The next day she came to me and said, "I prayed the prayer in that pamphlet and committed my life to Christ last night and today I feel great!" She has been growing in her newfound relationship with Christ ever since, and often relates how life is so different for her since that "day of decision." She came to me recently saying, "I need to ask you something. Am I okay or *nuts?* It's a funny thing,

but I am only in my mid-fifties and my thoughts regarding life in this world are changing. They are different than they were before all of this new life in Christ." And with tears of joy, she asked, "Is it normal to think that this world isn't really all there is? I seem to think that this is only so temporary and I am really beginning to look forward to heaven. I am not depressed or anything, but I've been reading a book and going to a Bible study that is helping me to understand purpose in life, and I don't think this earthly life is all there is."

I told her that I often hear my eighty-seven-year-old mother singing, "This world is not my home I'm just a passin' through. If heaven's not my home, then Lord, what will I do?"

The believer can confidently prepare for that "abundant entrance into glory" (2 Peter 1:11, KJV) and do so without remorse or regret. If we are living a life that honors the One who created us, He will bring us honor and respect that goes above anything that we could imagine, even after our return to dust. This perspective, in comparison to that of man's thinking which causes him to try to prolong life and reverse aging, gives a different view of illness, the changes and decline in health and abilities, as well as impending death in the older years.

I think that Wes Kuhrt must have lived each day of his life as if it were his last. From the beginning Adam had to make a choice: to rely upon God or himself. Man's trust in himself is self-reliant, unreliable, and shortsighted with respect to life, and he relies on his own strength rather than the One who has "breathed life into him." All the self-effort comes to nothing in the end.

Success or SUCCESS?

Man can never be satisfied with earthly pursuits. He seeks a higher purpose in life that can only be found in God. (See Ecclesiastes 3:11-15.) As I write, Chuck Colson, known for his role in Watergate and conversion to Christ that led him to found Prison Fellowship just died. In a re-run of an interview that I heard on the radio, he said, "I had everything that life could offer: I had a position of power; I was one of the closest people to the President of the United States; I ran the successful campaign that got him elected for a second term. I left the position to return to my law practice and the next morning I woke up and felt this tremendous emptiness inside."

> Man can never be satisfied with earthly pursuits because He seeks a higher purpose which can only be found in God.

We cannot find God's purpose by our own efforts but only as we enter into a relationship with Him and seek His direction in our lives. (3:19-22.) Otherwise, "all is vanity" (everything is meaningless), because we "all go to one place; all are from the dust, and all return to dust." Life is futile without God, for with death, the Spirit is stripped of the body; leaving the body to return to dust and the spirit to return to God. Then the judgment, "For God will bring every work into judgment, including every secret thing, whether good or evil" (12: 7, 14).

Man has eternity in his heart because God breathed into his nostrils the breath of life. He can't find true purpose or finish well unless he establishes a relationship with God through Jesus Christ. Once that relationship is established, man's desire should then be to cultivate it until it becomes the most important thing in his life.

9

Then as age progresses, the desire to please God and to be with God becomes foremost in his life. Like Wes Kuhrt, the godly older adult can live every day of his life as if it were his last day. This enables a person to finish well.

Why Do People Get Old?

I heard a speaker relate the following story a number of years ago. He was a speaker at a conference and someone stopped him in the hallway and asked, "Why do people get old?" This was a difficult time in his life since he had just buried his thirty-year-old son. It was probably the first thought that came to his mind and out from his lips. "So they can get ready to die!" He went on to say something like this: *My son, in his thirties, just died. I think if God had come and asked him if he was ready to come to heaven, he probably would have said, "No! No, I am not ready quite yet; I would like to do some things, see some things, and accomplish some things in my life—no, not now…a little later, please.*

Jealous for Heaven

As we age and have to deal with all kinds of struggles, the loss of friends, physical and mental losses—the blessings that await us in glory begin to look very inviting. There's an anticipation and desire for heaven. The speaker said that he had reflected upon his answer, and the more he thought about it—the more he believed that he was right. Why do people get old? So that they can get ready to die!

> As we age and have to deal with all kinds of struggles, the loss of friends, physical and mental losses—the blessings that await us in glory begin to look very inviting.

I remember a lady named Agnes who lived at Elim Park. I was fairly new in my ministry as the chaplain, and was conducting a funeral service in our chapel. In those days it was a common practice to have a funeral service with the casket present, and to have a calling hour prior to the service to pay respects and visit with the family. The residents of the home were coming in and making their way to the front of the chapel to view the body before finding their seats for the service. I was in the back, talking with the staff of the funeral home, when Agnes went up to the casket, took the hand of her friend, and began to wail, "Oh Lord, if only it were me…If only I could go home to glory…Oh yes, I would be so glad…Oh Lord, how happy she must be…If only it were me… Take me home, dear Lord!"

About then, one of the funeral home staff members said to me, "Is she all right?" To which I answered, "Yes, she's just jealous for heaven!" She was ready and waiting for the Lord to take her home as she was struggling through the ninth decade of her life.

Creation and Then Life

The Scriptures tell us that the making of man had two parts: 1) he was made from the dust of the ground; and 2) God breathed into his nostrils the breath of life. Charles G. Oakes said, "He became a living soul (Genesis 2:7b) and within the soul are to be found the unique qualities that mirror the image of God. The original account of the creation distinguishes between the body and the soul. The body is from the dust of the earth, the soul is from God Himself, and this distinction is kept up throughout the Bible and explained as different substances and different origins. The body shall return to dust, says the wise man, and the spirit shall return to God who gave it. Man is part of a grand plan that includes

his physical deterioration and death."[4] Perhaps with this in mind, the Apostle Paul writes in 2 Corinthians 4:16, "Therefore, we do not lose heart. Even though our outward man is perishing, yet the inward man is being renewed day by day." It is interesting that the NIV uses the phrase "is wasting away while the NASV says, "is decaying." Either way, the image is pretty graphic.

Man was created with honor and dignity in the image of God, and he is to live out his days with purpose, reflecting the image and likeness of God to the very last breath. The physical family and the church family are very important to the successful finish of man's life. A relationship with God will give inner strength to meet the demands of the changes, challenges, and crises of the aging process, and the presence of family, as well as the church family, should bring the encouragement and support needed to go through all of the circumstances of earthly life.

> Man was created with honor and dignity in the image of God, and he is to live out his days with purpose, reflecting the image and likeness of God to the very last breath.

The Bridge of Eternal Significance

Early in my ministry to older adults, God gave me a picture of man's life span from earth to eternity as pictured in the diagram below.

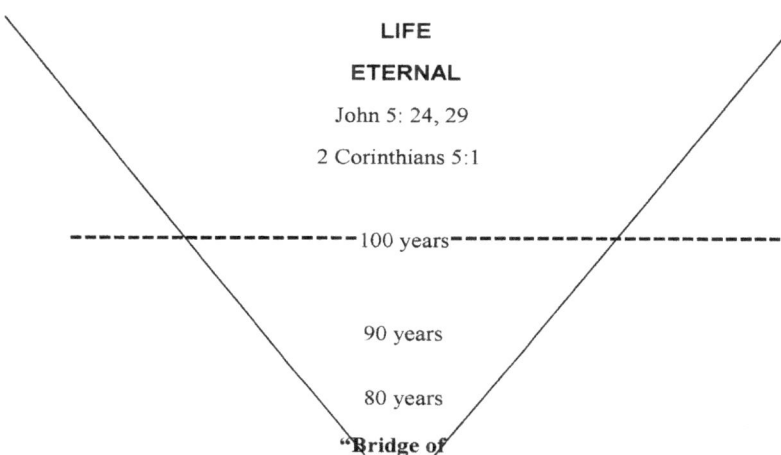

LIFE

ETERNAL

John 5: 24, 29

2 Corinthians 5:1

------------------------- 100 years ----------------------

90 years

80 years

"Bridge of

Psalm 90:10 "the number of our days will be seventy or if by strength eighty years…"

Eternal Significance"

70 years

60 years

-------------------------- 50 years ----------------------

LIFE

EXPERIENCE

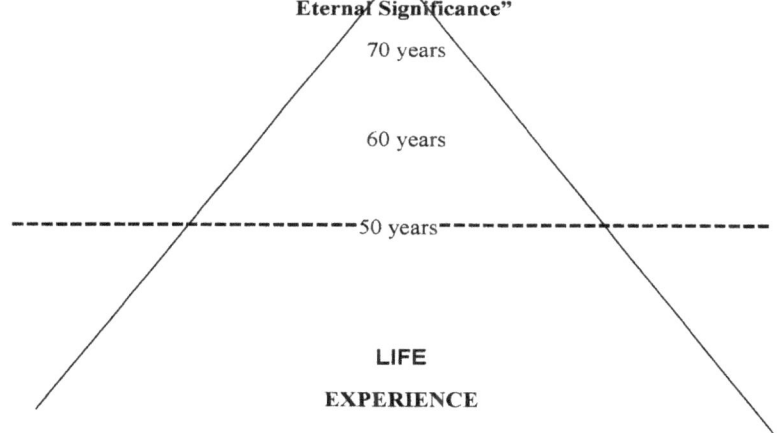

Bridge of Eternal Significance

All older adults are at an extremely strategic place regarding their spiritual lives. I like to visualize it as a "crossroad" or a "bridge" that I call, *"The bridge of eternal significance!"* It is that point where the arms of an X cross each other at the middle. As older adults look backward in their *life review,* the opening of the x on the bottom

13

represents the major portion of their *life experience*. It represents their life—including family (and other relationships), church, education, social life, work, world events, accomplishments, personality, etc. Social scientists and others describe this "life experience" that is relegated to the lower section of the x, as a life span of stages and ages. It is creatively described in many different ways in the literature of social scientists and researchers. Some describe *linear events* that occur at certain ages and periods of life while others picture a more *cyclic* order of events. A multitude of quotes give a humorous side to the aging process. Let me share some great illustrations of this.

Richard Morgan, a retired Presbyterian minister and a national leader in the life-review movement, tells the following story. "A rural woman with little education was overwhelmed at the thought of writing her life story, though she wanted to do so, badly. He suggested that she develop a theme. She came back with an outline:

Thrills (her parents at her birth)… Spills… Drills… Bills… Ills… Pills…Wills."[5]

Here are some other views of life development found in the pages of a book of illustrations that I find quite insightful and amusing.

"The Seven Stages of Man:
1. Milk
2. Milk, vegetables
3. Milk, ice cream sodas, candy
4. Steak, Coke, French fries, ham and eggs
5. Frogs' legs, caviar, Crepe Suzettes, Champagne
6. Milk and crackers
7. Milk"

Life's Key Words:

        1 - 20 years - learning
        20 - 30 years - ladies
        30 - 40 years - living
        40 - 50 years - liberty
        50 - 60 years - leisure
        60 - 70 years - living (or perhaps, lounging)

Life Strings:

    Apron Strings
    Heart Strings
    Purse Strings
    Harp Strings

The Chinese apply certain terms to different stages by naming each decade.
The age of:

        ten is called the opening degree;
        twenty, youth expired;
        thirty, strength and marriage;
        forty, officially apt;
        fifty, error-knowing;
        sixty, cycle-closing;
        seventy, rare bird of age;
        eighty, rusty-visaged;
        ninety, delayed;
        one hundred, age's extremity.

Life's Viewpoints:

    the old believe everything;
    the middle–aged suspect everything;

the young know everything.

The Sphinx Riddle supposedly dates back to ancient mythology but still carries truth today.

"What animal goes on four legs in the morning, on two at noonday, and on three in the evening? The riddle remained unsolved till Oedipus appeared and gave the right answer –**Man.** In infancy the human babe goes on all fours; during life's course he walks upright on two legs; and in the eventide of life he leans on a staff.

"Little Man" to "Old Gentleman"

In his essay *Three Score and Ten,* Stephen Leacock wrote about reaching seventy.

"The path through life from youth to age, you may trace for yourself by the varying way in which strangers address you. You begin as "little man," then "little boy" (because a little man is littler than a little boy), then "sonny," then "my boy," and after that "young man" and presently the interlocutor is younger than yourself and says, "Say, mister." I can still recall the thrill of pride I felt when a Pullman porter first called me "doctor" and when another raised me to "judge" and then the terrible shock it was when a taximan swung open his door and said, "step right in, Dad." Presently, I shall be introduced as "this venerable old gentleman" and the ax will fall when they raise me to the degree of "grand old man." That means, on our continent, anyone with snow–white hair who has kept out of jail till 80. That's the last and the worst they can do to you."

At the beginning of this century, there lived a Christian philosopher named Joseph Cook. He gave a summary of human life as follows:

"Man's life means
Tender teens,
Teachable twenties,
Tireless thirties,
Fiery forties,
Forceful fifties,
Serious sixties.
Sacred seventies.
Aching eighties,
Shortening breath,
Death.
The sod.
God!" [6]

Eternity Will Be Spent *Somewhere!*

The Bible says that the average life span lasts seventy to eighty years (Psalm 90:10), so the crossing point would represent those years. We know that death may take place right on schedule at seventy or eighty years or someplace before or after. So I simply put, a range of twenty years on either side, between the dotted lines, extending the years from fifty to hundred years, what some call the "second half of life." I would see the years of *Life Experience* (at the bottom of the **X**) as representing a time of preparation for the crossing of this critical bridge to eternity; this is where we cross from *Life Experience to Life Eternal.* As these years between the dotted lines represent the second half (age fifty until God calls a person home), it should be a time of contribution toward our

life eternal preparing for eternity, serving the God of eternity and assisting others to find their way to eternal life. They should be the years of significance; a time to evaluate our life and to make sure that our eternity will be spent in the presence of God in heaven rather than separated from God in hell. Keep in mind *we will all spend eternity somewhere!*

Some in the older adult field talk about conscious aging, but not in the sense that we have described above. A consciousness of eternity will guide a person during life here on earth to do so with heaven in mind (Colossians 3: 1-3). What a tremendous challenge for the older adult and those of us who are called to minister to them.

In the next chapter, I will begin to develop a short theology of aging with the outline that follows: *Respected, Rejected,* and the Need to be *Re-connected.* Much of my experience has come through involvement in ministry to those in the categories of retired life (sixty five to eighty years) and senior life (eighty plus), as a chaplain in a continuing care retirement community, as well as involvement in the leadership team of a denominational and district ministry mentioned already. I do hope that when you finish this book, though, that you will have been exposed to enough Scripture to develop your own personal Bible-based theology about aging. I pray that this study will not only bring about an awareness of a biblical calling to serve this generation, but a sensitivity to care for and challenge this group of adults over age fifty-five as you minister to and through them.

Reflect and Grow

- *Where are you personally in this aging process? What insights would you share with those who follow after you?*

- *Considering your own journey, what mark have you left on the world? What legacy will you leave behind?*
- *How would you describe your own aging process?*
- *What can you do to improve this process?*

Chaper two

Respected

Recognizing the special place that mankind has been given, compared to the rest of creation, it is no wonder that God would value and respect man throughout his lifetime. Leviticus 19:32 points out that those with gray heads, those who are older, deserve respect and honor: "You shall rise before the gray headed and honor the presence of an old man, and fear your God: I am the LORD." This verse links our respect for the older generation to our own relationship with God. Out of reverence and worship of God we give honor the older person. Oates writes, "Throughout the Bible, seniority entitles people to respect, and a long life is seen as bringing experience and wisdom together."[7]

Respect for parents is noted in Leviticus 19:3 which says, "Every one of you shall revere his mother and his father..." The Fifth Commandment is the only one with an attached promise as parents are given respect: "Honor your father and your mother, that your days may be long upon the land which the LORD your God is giving you" (Exodus 20:12). Other Old Testament scripture verses that speak of honor and respect for parents and older adults are found in Proverbs and Job. "Grandchildren are the crown of the aged, and the glory of children is their fathers" (Proverbs 17:6,

ESV). We also read, "Listen to your father who gave you life, and do not despise your mother when she is old" (Proverbs 23:22, ESV).

In the book of Job a verse introduces us to a younger man named Elihu thinks he knows the answers to Jobs problems but does not want to show disrespect by seeming to know more than Job, his elder, without gaining Job's permission to speak. "So Elihu, the son of Barachel the Buzite, answered and said, 'I *am* young in years, and you *are* very old; therefore I was afraid, and dared not declare my opinion to you'" (Job 32:6).

Gray Hair Does Not Always Equate to Wisdom

Look at the next verse, "I said, 'Age should speak, and multitude of years should teach wisdom'" (32:7). As one reads the Scriptures it is assumed that wisdom comes with older age. That seems logical, but we should not accept the fact that just because a person has gray hair that person is wise. "Multitude of years *should* (italics mine) teach wisdom." True wisdom and knowledge, says Proverbs 1:7, comes with the fear (reverence, awe) of the Lord. True wisdom only comes from a relationship with God through faith in Jesus Christ.

Rather than making fun of old age, scripture respects the attainment of old age. Proverbs 16:31 (ESV) says, "Gray hair is a crown of glory; it is gained in a righteous life", and 20:29 goes on to say, "The glory of young men is their strength, and the splendor of old men is their gray head."

In Genesis 9:20-27 a story speaks of the respect that ought to be given to parents as well as all older adults. These verses relate the account of Noah becoming drunk as he drank too much fermented juice from his vineyard of grapes. Noah's youngest son found

him lying naked and drunk in his tent. Upon seeing his father's condition he went and told his older brothers to come and look. Rather than look upon their father's condition, they backed into the tent and covered him up with a blanket, so as not to look upon him in his compromised state. The youngest son, Ham and his future generations were cursed due to such terrible disrespect for his father; whereas the older two brothers, and their generations, received the blessing of their father. How we as adults treat our parents can affect how our children will show respect and honor for us as we age.

Several years ago, in our church newsletter to the older adult group called the Evergreens, an article appeared titled *Wise Master Builders,* attributed to John Gillmartin in *Sermon Illustrations Each Week.*

"The story is told of a frail old man who went to live with his son, daughter-in-law and four-year-old grandson. The old man's hands trembled, his eyesight was blurred, and his step faltered. Each night the family ate their evening meal together and the old man's hands shook. This, combined with his failing sight, made eating difficult. Peas rolled off his fork; when he grasped the glass, milk spilled out; and he often dropped things on his way to the table.

The son and daughter-in-law became increasingly irritated with the mess. "We must do something about Grandfather," said the son. "I've had enough of his spilled milk, noisy eating, and food on the floor," said the daughter-in-law. So they set a small table in the corner of the kitchen, over the linoleum. Their Grandfather ate alone, while the "family" enjoyed dinner together. And when Grandfather had little to say, and the only words the couple said to him were admonitions to be careful and not make a mess. The four-year-old watched in silence.

One evening before supper, the father noticed his son playing with scrap wood on the kitchen floor. He asked his child, "What are you making?" The boy responded, "I'm making two little bowls, one for you and for mama to use when you get old after I grow up."

Needless to say, grandpa made a speedy return to the dinner table. For the remainder of his life with them, they ate their meals as a family; and for some reason, no one seemed to care when a fork was dropped, or milk was spilled, or the tablecloth became soiled.

Children are remarkably aware: their eyes see, their ears hear, and their minds process. If they observe a happy family home, they'll imitate that for the rest of their lives. The wise parent realizes that every day is a building day and the foundation is being laid for the child's future."

Honor Is More Than Respect

The New Testament also calls us to honor our parents, and in general, all older adults. Honor is more than showing respect, saying kind words and being polite; honor requires action and participation in their lives. In Ephesians 6:1-3 the command says, "Children, obey your parents in the Lord, for this is right. *Honor your father and mother, that it may be well with you and you may live long on the earth."* This is the only commandment that carries a promise! The honoring of parents still holds for all adult children. The commandment is active as long as parents are alive.

> Honor is more than showing respect, saying kind words and being polite; honor requires action and participation in their lives.

Paul instructs a young pastor, "Do not rebuke an older man but encourage him as you would a father. Treat younger men like brothers, older women like mothers, younger women like sisters, in all purity. *Honor widows who are truly widows"* (1 Timothy 5:1-3, ESV and italics are mine added for emphasis). It is apparent that it is the older widows that need care from the church body, especially if there are no children or grandchildren. "But if a widow has children or grandchildren, let them first learn to show godliness to their own household and to make some return to their parents, for this is pleasing in the sight of God. She who is truly a widow, left all alone, has set her hope on God and continues in supplications and prayers night and day" (4-5, ESV).

The importance of the family, intended by God from the beginning of mankind, is illustrated in these verses and gives to us another reminder that the way we treat older adults is a reflection of our relationship and service to God.

Paul reminded Timothy that there is a pastoral and a church responsibility to the widow of older age in 1 Timothy 5:9-11. "Do not let a widow under sixty years old be taken into the number, and not unless she has been the wife of one man, well reported for good works: if she has brought up children, if she has lodged strangers, if she has washed the saints' feet, if she has relieved the afflicted, if she has diligently followed every good work. But refuse the younger widows; for when they have begun to grow wanton against Christ, they desire to marry."

Perhaps some of the widows, with certain qualifications as defined in these verses, were doing work for the church in exchange for some financial support. When the widows lose the most significant person in their lives for emotional and financial support, it is great

if the church can help them find purpose, using their maturity and wisdom in service to the local body of Christ.

There is a strong call to the church family to care for the widows in James 1:27, "Pure and undefiled religion before God and the Father is this: to *visit* orphans and *widows* in their trouble, *and* to keep oneself unspotted from the world." This differs from the Old Testament in which the widows were to be cared for by the Levites and not by the whole congregation of people. [8]

The church that my wife and I attended for several years scheduled a Sunday worship service each November to honor the widows and widowers of the congregation. My family became familiar with this idea when we were traveling through Virginia on a Sunday morning and visited a Baptist church. The congregation hosted a special annual event to honor the older adult widows and widowers. We were blessed as the Pastor and leaders honored the widows and widowers during that Sunday morning worship service. They were asked to stand and received honor with the applause of the congregation. A photo of each was taken as they were presented with a gift of flowers and a gift certificate to a local restaurant.

The pastor used the occasion, through the preaching of the Word, to teach his congregation about their responsibility to care for the widows and widowers. He reminded the people that though we, as Christian believers, are careful to honor mothers and fathers on a special day of the year, the care of widows sets a higher Biblical distinctive. It is the way that we express *pure and undefiled religion.*

Our family was deeply moved by this expression of Biblical care for those older adults of the congregation and when we arrived home, we brought the idea to our pastor and church leaders. We added a special Sunday to honor widows and widowers and it became an

annual event for several years. I was touched one Sunday, as I filled the pulpit in a local church, to hear a leader pray specifically by name for the needs of two widows in the congregation.

May is nationally designated as *older adult month* and our church also set apart an *Older Adult Sunday* to honor all seniors in the congregation. With that theme of the day, the worship service included songs, scriptures, and responsive readings that were their favorites and the sermon spoke of the church's responsibility toward older adults. The older members shared testimonies and presented the special music of the service. The leader of this ministry usually preached the sermon on that day and challenged the congregation to provide honor and care to these treasures. The message also included a challenge to the older adults, to *finish well.*

It is interesting that many of the covenants in the Old Testament affirm the important role of the older adults.

"The part played by the elderly in bringing God's sovereign will to pass cannot be easily dismissed. In every generation of mankind and under every covenant, the old and their wisdom are foundational for social stability and continuity. The history of those of advancing age is coterminous with God's history. Leaders have come, ruled well or badly, and passed on, but a hallmark of God's plan has been righteous men and women of old age.

It is not coincidental that God chose aged Abraham and Sarah as the vehicles through whom to bless all nations; or Noah who labored for 120 years merely to make the ark; or Moses who began the forty year journey into the wilderness when he was a mere lad of eighty; or weakened, shriveled, and infirmed Simeon and Anna to be the first outside of Joseph's family to proclaim Jesus in the temple as the Salvation of the Lord and the one through whom

the New Covenant was established; and John, then over 100 years old, to be the revelator who saw Jesus in the heavens as the Lion of Judah and the slain Lamb of God, worthy to open the Scroll, read the judgment of the universe, and usher in the *parousia* of all time. God's written plan, purpose, and history have among the common threads, a special deliberate place for the hoary heads—those of advancing years. Not the young and strong but the old, wise, and seasoned. The covenants were introduced on seasoned shoulders, bent perhaps, but deliberate and given to the long view.

God has a vital place for those of His children who remain righteous in their later years…It concerns the righteous in whom the sap continues to flow and the fruit continues to yield. Hence, the theology of the advancing years becomes an object lesson for those of younger years who themselves will, through time, ascend to those exalted places in their own generation."[9]

Let's look at Leviticus to get a clearer understanding regarding the value of man in his older years.

"Of course, the Biblical accounts recognized that there was a diminishing contribution the aged could make. There is a discussion, in the book of Leviticus (27:3, 7) as to how much a man shall pay when he vows his own value to God. Men pledged to God a variety of gifts: livestock, children, as with Hannah and Samuel, and themselves. If a man vowed himself to God, what was his obligation in monetary terms? For a man in the prime of life, the obligation was fifty shekels.

At age sixty, however, the valuation dropped to fifteen. The important point is that it never dropped to zero; a human being had value, no matter what the number of years reached. The aged must have been honored to be numbered among the elders who

sat at the gate to be called upon by the virtue of their age, their dignity, and their experience to act as witnesses to agreements, juries in lawsuits, and advisers on matters of public concern. In our day, however, old age is not so much a blessing as it is a problem. At one time they would have been the elders; now they are the elderly. The elderly, well or ill, need the self-respect that derives from being usefully occupied, if possible, and warmly cared for. They need relationships with God, with self, and with community, which nurtures them in their old age."[10]

> **God has given a wonderful promise to older adults who have earned respect and honor; for they heard His voice, discovered their purpose and walked with Him throughout their lives.**

God has given a wonderful promise to older adults who have earned respect and honor; for they heard His voice, discovered their purpose and walked with Him throughout their lives.

Read this promise and commit it to memory as you think of the older adults or parent(s) under your care, and then let it be the reminder that you will need as you age. "Even to your old age, I am He. And even to gray hairs I will carry you! I have made, and I will bear; even I will carry, and will deliver *you*" (Isaiah 46:4).

Finishing well! This verse in Isaiah indicates the best way to get there is supported by the strong arms of the Father, who desires the privilege and responsibility to carry the trusting older adult securely in His arms, through earthly living…and all the way to eternity.

Reflect and Grow

- *How can you help the older adult in your church have this kind of assurance?*

- *In general, how do we treat the senior adults in this country? While you cannot singlehandedly change the world, what can you do for the senior who sits beside you at church or the one that lives next door?*

- *How can we honor our parents and the seniors around us?*

Chapter Three

Rejected

Though the Old and New Testaments uphold the honor and respect of the older adult, we see the beginning of the rejection of the older adult in 1 Kings 12. King Rehoboam was trying to decide how to treat King Jeroboam and the ten tribes of Israel. In the heavy building programs of his father, King Solomon, the people had become exhausted, drained, and were looking for a little reprieve from the heavy commitments that they were called upon to support in Solomon's aggressive and burdensome undertakings. In 1 Kings 12:3, the people said to the king, "Your father made our yoke heavy; therefore, lighten the burdensome service of your father, and his heavy yoke which he put on us, and we will serve you." The King consulted with the older men, the elders, (vs. 6) and they, with their wisdom, told him what to do, "And they spoke to him, saying, "If you will be a servant to these people today, and serve them, and answer them, and speak good words to them, then they will be your servants forever" (1 Kings 12:7).

For some reason, perhaps pride, he did not like their advice and consulted the younger men, of his own age, ignoring the wisdom of the old: "But he *rejected the advice* which the elders had given him and consulted the young men who had grown up with him, who

stood before him" (1 Kings 12:8, italics are added to give emphasis to thoughts about older adults).

"Then the king *answered the people roughly,* and *rejected the advice* which the elders had given him; and he spoke to them according to the advice of the young men, saying, "My father made your yoke heavy, but I will add to your yoke; my father chastised you with whips, but I will chastise you with scourges" (1 Kings 12:13-14).

Consider 1 Peter 5:5b, "…for 'God resists the proud, but gives grace to the humble.'" Proverbs 16:18 gives the outcome of pride. "Pride *goes* before destruction, and a haughty spirit before a fall." Rejecting the wisdom of the older men resulted in division—the division of the kingdom—which lasted for centuries.

Worship May Create Contention

Many leaders in the church today reject the wisdom and advice of the older adults and the result is often that of division. One area of contention so prevalent in many churches today is in the area of worship. The subject comes up often in my conversation with older adults.

> **When the worship leader is pressured to increase membership through a dynamic music program, little concern is shown to the seniors.**

Rather than being sensitive to the older adults and their desires for worship, many of the younger leaders are apt to say, "Get with the program; we have to reach the present generation so live with it!" Perhaps an opportunity to discuss the subject of worship, and the needs of the different age groups within the congregation would

bring a better understanding between all. When the worship leader is pressured to increase membership through a dynamic music program designed for reaching the younger generation with little concern shown to the seniors. The battle begins as the older folks in the church dig their heels in and stop trying to understand what the younger generation wants or needs as they worship. Communication shuts down and frustration and hurt begins to surface. Some "give and take" needs to accommodate one another in a way that honors God and carries a concern for the needs of each generation into the worship service. I have visited churches where this has happened in a God honoring, Holy Spirit directed way.

Recently in my devotions I came across 1 Peter 5:5-6, which reads, "Likewise you younger people, submit yourselves to *your* elders. Yes, all of *you* be submissive to one another, and be clothed with humility, for "God resists the proud, But gives grace to the humble. Therefore humble yourselves under the mighty hand of God, that He may exalt you in due time." It was not but a short time later that same day when God brought me to Ephesians 5:18b -20, "but be filled with the Spirit, speaking to one another in psalms and hymns and spiritual songs, singing and making melody in your heart to the Lord, giving thanks always for all things to God the Father in the name of our Lord Jesus Christ."

I believe that the Holy Spirit impressed upon me something that I had never seen in that verse before. Combined with 1 Peter 5:5-6, the verse seemed to say to me: If we are filled with the Holy Spirit then the outcome will be *speaking to one another;* speaking to one another with humility rather than prideful desires that keep both young and old from hearing each other. The verse is speaking about music as it indicates, "psalms and hymns and spiritual songs." In the music of the church, God seems to have

given Paul, by inspiration, the formula for settling the issue of the music in the church through out history. In our day, perhaps it speaks about a blended service that brings in the "one another" principles that ought to characterize our Christian lives into the worship. Honoring God and one another with songs of worship that minister in a wonderful way to one another is what it is all about.

Worship Doesn't Change - Style Changes

It is my observation that there is little "give and take" in most worship services. It is a one-way-or-the-highway type of attitude that excludes the wishes and desires of those who would like to worship with the music that is meaningful to the different generations. If the Holy Spirit is alive and well and if there is a spirit of humility, it seems like God's Word assures a worshipful and meaningful sensing of His grace. This should work in a way that allows all present to give thanks in their hearts as they make melody to God in the name of the Lord Jesus Christ.

While living in another state, my wife and I visited a church that was made up of a large number of people who had immigrated to the United States from another country. The church was named for that group and eventually became The Church of all Nations as it began to grow. It was an interesting group of people who had more of a charismatic desire for worship than those who were more conservative in their style of worship. The pastor was not really charismatic but he welcomed and allowed the charismatic pianist to guide the opening part of the worship of the church from the piano. It still remains one of the most unique churches I have visited because the people loved and enjoyed one another, loved their pastor, and had a worship service that was awe-inspiring; and

the church grew. From time to time, we enjoyed the worship that was quite refreshing and uplifting. They seemed to be able to put to practice the instruction of Peter and Paul, and humbly serve each other.

Finished and Fed Up

The daughter of one of our residents related her personal experience to me. Her story saddened me as I heard her describe what seemed to be such insensitivity to one who had faithfully served the Lord and her church in the music ministry for over forty-five years. She was not treated with honor or respect. This woman had played the piano and organ in the church from her teen years. Now in her sixties, the new worship minister abruptly told her one Sunday that her services were no longer needed because his wife was accomplished on the keyboard and they were changing the style of worship. Furthermore, the keyboard (and his wife) would immediately replace the use of the organ and piano. It happened quickly, with no preparation, and that was it!

> Many pastors have become so concerned about reaching the un-churched that they are "un-churching" the churched!"

The organist and her husband requested a meeting with the pastor and the deacons, and their son also attended. The son verified that the meeting progressed as follows. The pastor was preoccupied during most of the discussion in the meeting, and when he was asked for his thoughts, he replied sleepily, "If you're upset and want to leave—it's okay, for we would rather keep the younger people than the older ones!" Can you imagine the hurt

34

that was experienced by that couple with such insensitivity that came from the pastor—of *all* people? Needless to say they did leave, after being a part of that church that they loved and served for over sixty years. They now belong to another church where they have found a place of service and ministry, and are greatly appreciated. In fact, they have revitalized the music and spiritual life of their new church.

It may be that things needed to change. However, I think if the reasons for change were given in a friendly discussion instead of the abrupt actions of the new worship minister, this couple might have come on board and supported the ministry that had effectively grown over the years. It bothers me deeply to hear of such insensitivity in the place where things should be different.

In a newsletter called *Milk and Honey* I found an interesting article on the value of age that states, "Nowhere in Scripture are elders ever described as retiring or urged to do so." The question was asked a few sentences later, "Why then is there so much talk today about the need for older men to step aside and to turn God's work over to younger men? Is it because older men are no longer wise? Or is it because changes are desired which age and wisdom might not approve."[11]

In an article titled *Older Christians are Leaving Churches* by Wayne J. Edwards, he referred to a report on the webpage of his denomination that said, "Today's young adults are less likely than any other age group to attend church, read the Bible or donate to religious causes, especially if they do not feel a personal connection to the ministry." The article then went on to say that the church had better change the way it relates to younger members and find some way to connect with them, because 'they won't buy into the same old, same old'." The author indicates that the church should

not direct its whole concern to this group and the un-churched while it allows, and even encourages, those who have been involved in the church with their time, talent, and tithes for years to check out.

Many times these older faithful servants are told in no uncertain terms that they need to move over and make room for a new generation. *And to offer any criticism* at all *is to question the will of God.* He goes on to say that many pastors have become so concerned about reaching the un-churched that they are "un-churching" the churched! "And it seems," he says, "like they are afraid to ask them why they are leaving. Those who are writing the contemporary church growth manuals," he says, "are saying the old disciplines of inductive Bible study, dynamic expository preaching, and the great hymns of our faith, are actually barriers to unbelievers—hindrances that must be removed if we are to reach a new generation of lost people." He concludes that the faithful remnant, those who sacrificed time, talents, and tithes to see the church begin, grow and develop, are now being relegated to the rear of the sanctuary, or they are being told to leave, systematically removed as those who no longer matter.[12]

Perhaps David felt the rejection of age, too, when he remembered his past participation of worship at the temple and apparently was not able to do so any more: "When I remember these *things,* I pour out my soul within me. For I used to go with the multitude; I went with them to the house of God, with the voice of joy and praise, with a multitude that kept a pilgrim feast" (Psalm 42:4). In the next verse he expresses his discouragement at feeling rejected, and yet seems to know that his hope is to be found only in God when he is feeling like this. "Why are you cast down, O my soul? And *why* are you disquieted within me? Hope in God, for I shall yet praise Him *for* the help of His countenance" (42:5). He goes on to

remind himself that though he feels rejected and left out, a feeling that may seem to be highlighted in the quietness of the night time, he will hear God's song, "…And in the night His song will be with me" (Psalm 42:8).

When we were expecting our third child, there was a new theory that was making the baby circuit. Based upon one teaching that I had heard, I would often put my mouth close to my wife's tummy and sing to him. I continued singing the familiar words of the hymn, *Jesus Loves Me This I Know* until he was born. After his birth, whenever he was "disquieted" I would sing Jesus Loves Me, and he would seem to quiet down and find rest. I can't help but be drawn to the verse that reminds me that my heavenly Father rejoices over me with singing. When He thinks about me, He breaks into singing (and perhaps a little dancing too)! Oh, how that must rest the soul. I can't help but think if the voice of this earthly father could bring such quietness to his infant with singing, how much more the song of our Heavenly Father?

Look at Zephaniah 3:17, "The LORD your God in your midst, the Mighty One, will save; he will rejoice over you with gladness, he will quiet you with His love, he will rejoice over you with singing." When the feeling of rejection begins to rise in the life of the older adult, he must quickly turn to the only place for hope and recognition—God, who will show his loving kindness.

Our attitude toward older adults that are shut-in or unable to be active anymore, may cause them to feel like they have lost the respect and honor that would make them feel like a valued part of the congregation. This can lead to the feeling of being forgotten and rejected. They are not sought out for advice anymore; others think their thoughts to be old fashioned; and their input is often rejected and no longer desired.

Integration and Wholeness

An important part of therapy for older adults in nursing homes, and a natural happening as older adults try to find purpose and meaning in their lives is called *life review.* Erikson, describes *integration* as this eighth stage at sixty-five years and above. This is Erikson's final stage, that he calls "integrity versus despair." It is so named because the task

> **Failure to integrate the past, present, and future leaves one in disgust and despair: disgusted about the past, despairing about the present and discouraged (hopeless) concerning the future.**

at this time of life is to *integrate,* or to gather together a person's whole life; to come to terms with his personal past, present and future. Integration implies wholeness. It suggests that those who are successful at this stage are those who are content with who they are and have been. Failure to integrate the past, present, and future leaves one in disgust and despair: disgusted about the past, despairing about the present and discouraged (hopeless) concerning the future. David reviews God's involvement in his life and his own commitment to serve Him in Psalm 71:5-7. He expresses his hope and trust in the Lord using these words: "For You are my hope, O Lord GOD; *you are* my trust from my youth. By You I have been upheld from birth; You are He who took me out of my mother's womb. My praise *shall be* continually of You. I have become as a wonder to many, but You *are* my strong refuge."

Being human, David wonders if he will simply be put on the shelf and not appreciated anymore. "Do not cast me off in the time of old age; Do not forsake me when my strength fails. For my enemies speak against me; and those who lie in wait for my life take

counsel together, Saying, "God has forsaken him; Pursue and take him, for *there is* none to deliver *him*" (Psalm 71: 9 – 11).

Valid or Invalid?

In our western culture we place much emphasis and value upon youthfulness, competition, and self-dependence. I am glad that we no longer use the word "invalid" to speak of the elderly or others with special needs. When you break down the meaning of *invalid* it simply means *not valid,* and that is how we see many of our elderly people in the community, the church, and especially in nursing homes. For many, aging is thought of as a time of loss and decline.

In America, our emphasis is upon youthfulness! People who cannot show these youthful traits may find themselves being treated with intolerance, impatience, annoyance, hostility and rejection. Families, church members and people that have previously been a part of their lives distance themselves from these has-beens. Is it any wonder that depression is a common outcome in the lives of many older adults? As friends begin to die, or move away, there is a great danger of isolation.

Some years ago, someone gave me a paper by a person named David Davis, who at the time was the Protestant Chaplain at St. Elizabeth's Hospital in Washington, D.C. The paper presented a good understanding of the struggle that many elderly experience, not only as residents in nursing homes but in the community and church, as well. He saw the many fears and anxieties of the aged falling under four categories that he called *The Four D's* and they include Deterioration, Detachment, Deprivation, and Dependency. "What these people seem to be communicating cannot be said in better words than the Psalmist used many years ago, 'Do not cast me off in the time of old age; Do not forsake me…'" (Psalm 71:9).

I hear the Psalmist talking about fears of deterioration when he says, "When my strength fails"; talking about the fears of deprivation and detachment as he says, "Cast me not off"; talking about dependency as he says, "Forsake me not"; What the Psalmist seems to be conveying is the need for support and companionship."[13]

> Loss is one of the greatest things that older adults have to deal with in life.

Loss is one of the greatest things that older adults have to deal with in life. It doesn't matter whether it is in the community, a nursing home, or a continuing care retirement community, loss is still loss. I am not necessarily talking just about death because there are many kinds of losses in a senior's life. Loss of independence when they can no longer see well enough to drive, loss of muscle control to make it to the bathroom in time, loss of eye-hand coordination to feed themselves gracefully, loss of hearing etc., all fall under the same category as death.

At the Gerontology Forum, held in Boston in 1983, there is a reference to an article entitled, "Loss, Depletion and Restitution" in the book, *Geriatric Psychiatry* (International Universities Press, 1962). In an article titled, *Grief and Loss in the Aging Process,* Timothy J. Wildman quotes Cath who outlines four basic anchorages for mental health and emotional stability throughout the life cycle. "These are (1) self and body image, (2) acceptable home, (3) social and economic security and (4) meaningful purpose. The threat of loss or an actual loss in any one or more of these anchorages can produce a significant psychological reaction in the individual. While Dr. Wildman notes that this can happen to anyone, at any age, it is obvious that multiple losses in all four anchorages are much more common in the later years. As with a

boat, when the anchor is pulled, and it begins to drift and roll on the waves without direction, it can get lost at sea. So it is when an anchor is pulled in any one of the four areas above, it can lead to an aimless drifting, and a person's becoming lost in the confusion of life. The way in which a loss is perceived, or whether the event is perceived as a loss at all, is of great importance, for this colors the way in which a person adapts to the event. Losses from change in a job, a relationship, health, mental ability, housing, and a host of other things only increase as the years are added."[14]

Drifting in Unchartered Waters

In God's Word we find a reminder to those older adults to whom we minister and for those who are reaching out to Jesus in times when they feel like they are adrift. "We have strong consolation, who have fled for refuge to lay hold of the hope set before *us*. This *hope* (Jesus) we have as an anchor of the soul, both sure and steadfast…" (Hebrews 6:18-19).

The church needs to respect, to be supportive, and not reject the needs of the older adults. One pastor, in one of our denominational churches, told his congregation from the pulpit that the church would *not* provide for the needs of older adults. The church was seeking to bring in younger families, and his comment went something like this, "You older folks have been around for a long time and have been through many experiences. You have learned to cope with life so you can handle things on your own. We aren't going to provide programming and be concerned about your needs; you're old enough to take care of yourselves." What can possibly be more hurtful than words such as these? It would be like telling them that they were welcome to keep their boat anchored in the harbor but no one would be coming to rescue them if a storm came along.

Another pastor once said to me, as I was leading him to the part of our facility where his church member resided, "Have you ever thought about starting your own church here?"

> I am firmly rooted in reality and understand that senior's ministry is not for everyone but unfortunately, everyone will be a senior one day.

I asked him, "Why would I want to do that?"

He sighed and quickly replied, "Then I would not have to come and do this; you could do it for me!"

I am firmly rooted in reality and understand that senior's ministry is not for everyone but unfortunately, everyone will be a senior one day. So let's have a little compassion here!

Shut Ins Are Shut Out

The western philosophy focus upon youthfulness has crept into the church and into the thinking of many pastors in not-so-subtle ways! The result has been to move away from shut-ins, especially nursing home residents to the point that they are often ignored and neglected.

Dr. Robert Butler, former Director of the National Center on Aging, shared some interesting yet sad statistics. He said that 95% of all nursing home residents never receive a visitor during the year, and that 85% never receive a meaningful piece of mail. These statistics may have changed over the years, but the situation is basically the same. I believe that there are many residents of nursing homes or retirement communities that have been forgotten by their clergy and their communities of worship.

A young pastor friend said to me one day, "If I were in your ministry I could only look at it as ushering people into heaven." My first thought was, "Aren't we in the same business?" He was a new pastor, having just graduated from seminary a few years before and was experiencing the excitement of a growing church with young people, and young families.

I guess the thought of my ministry did not sound too exciting to him, and perhaps in reality–quite boring! At that point, he really had not asked me anything about what I did. He just made an assumption. I understood what he was saying, but my inner response to his comment was, "Why should we make them walk alone?" My mind then did a crazy thing and I remembered the Apostle Paul's words in Romans 6:1. "What shall we say then? Shall we continue in sin, that grace may abound?" The answer to his own question is found in the next verse. "God forbid!" With a similar analogy, though out of context, I thought, "Are we making our elderly people feel so miserable, lonely, left out and forgotten that they will enjoy heaven more?" God forbid!

"Please, Won't You Just Come and Talk with Me?"

I remember the day that I walked through the hall to our skilled nursing facility and as I approached the lounge, I saw Mildred in a wheelchair sitting to the far side of the lounge. It looked like she was reaching out with her hand and as I got closer that is exactly what she was doing. Reaching out as if pointing at something with her fingers, she would turn her hand back toward herself, as if to wave someone to come to her. I went to her and asked her what she was doing. As she continued with the outstretched arm, pointing and motioning back toward her, she said, "I beckon with my finger for someone to come and talk to me and no one comes." My heart

was saddened for this resident who was longing for attention from someone.

She then said, "Won't you just kiss me before you go so that I would know that someone cares about me." Needless to say, I called the church to which she belonged, as well as family members, to say that she needed some added attention to help chase the loneliness away.

I often think of the words of a song that was written by a student of Barrington College in Barrington, Rhode Island. She had been doing an internship of visitation at a nursing home as a part of her course work, and expressed her thoughts in these moving words:

I know a lady, name of Mary,
A little lady with brown eyes.
In the city lived my Mary
Throughout her life, she'd there abide.

She had a husband, and a small house
Where she lived and loved and grew.
But no children came to Mary
And her husband is gone too.

There is a dark room, with two windows
That Mary looked out yesterday.
I went to see her for an hour
To chase the loneliness away.

But today they took Mary to the hospital
And they let me see her, because she had no family.
But Mary couldn't hear me…
So I just prayed and walked away.

I know a Lady, name of Mary,
For just an hour once a week.
How many Mary's are still waiting?
A little love is what they seek.

For they were young once, and they loved once
They were like us once – Just the same.
And they still need love, and they still give love…
If they are lonely – who's to blame.[15]

You cannot lump seniors together and make a general statement such as, "Oh, they are all just alike!" That is simply not the truth. Not all seniors age in the same way; their needs are different! They do *not* become more like one another as they age. There are some common changes in a general way, but each ages differently. The older a person becomes, the more losses they experience. The basic needs are for love and understanding from those who can exercise the love and compassion of Jesus Christ and it is up to those of us who serve and care for these older adults to find out what the needs are and how to meet them. Often what is needed is someone to listen and help them get those feelings sorted out.

Ageism

Ageism is very real. It's still unacceptable to be old in our culture! Our Western philosophy values youth and discredits old age. We are faced with this fact every day and we see it in television commercials with the advertising for anti-aging creams, in birthday cards that make fun of the limitations that sometimes accompany the aging process; and in conversations concerning our own aging.

In a recent magazine article telling of the use of Botox in the war against wrinkles, these words open up the humorous account, "As baby boomers age, they get older. But they don't necessarily want to look older. One of the signs of old age is wrinkles, those expressive crevices that reflect a lifetime of frowns or laughter." It then discusses the approval by the FDA in 1989 of the drug Botox for treating these wrinkles. The American Society for Aesthetic Plastic Surgery reports that hundreds of thousands of Americans have attacked their worry lines with very expensive treatments since then. "The lines elided by Botox also speak eloquently about American culture. Indeed, the crack research team of the American Studies Museum has concluded that Botox isn't the only toxin in this story. Instead, it's merely a pharmaceutical response to a toxic pattern in American culture, a pattern by which our denial of death and aging affects the living of our lives.

We naturally fear aging, infirmity, and death. But we culturally fear them too, in ways that other cultures don't. In the past, particularly people culturally contrived to make aging and death graceful, old people were respected as wise and experienced guides to life, not simply as old fogies." A few lines later it goes on to say, "Generally, it [advertising] informs us that we should look 20 or 21, or at least youthful. Many ads suggest that we should physically deny what is experientially true—we've been around for a while. They teach us that people will think less of us because we wear the signs of age." [16]

What can we say about the obsession with the need to be perfect? Billions of dollars are spent on perfect skin, hair, lips, eyelashes, noses, breasts and the list goes on. Obviously these focus on the externals in life but what about the internal or spiritual condition of man? After all the face lifts, tummy tucks and Botox treatments are completed, the reality still remains – we are headed toward one

of two places. How beautiful does one have to look to meet Jesus? Does He really care about the outward appearance of man? "But the LORD said to Samuel, "Do not look at his appearance or at his physical stature, because I have refused him. For the LORD does not see as man sees; for man looks at the outward appearance, but the LORD looks at the heart" (1 Samuel 16:7).

The Second Half

Hosea 7:9 says of Israel, "Aliens have devoured his strength, But he does not know it; *Yes, gray hairs are here and there on him, Yet he does not know it."* This describes some of those who enter into the "second half of life."

Some look at life as pictured on the bell curve; and because of the emphasis upon youthfulness come to the fortieth birthday with black balloons and a message of doom, because they feel that they have reached the apex of living and it is all down hill from there. I like to look at this thought with what I call "Schauffle's Shuffle." Dr. Schauffle was one of my professors when I was a student at Gordon-Conwell Theological Seminary. This diagram came from one of his Christian Education courses.

40 years old

<u>run</u>

/ \

<u>walk</u>   <u>walk</u>

/ \

/ \

schuffle   schuffle

/ \

/ \

Birth___crawl_/   \ crawl___**Death**

The downward side of the bell curve reverses backward to a "second childhood." This may be true as the year's mount up and the physical and mental abilities slow down. Nevertheless, the believer should be encouraged to "be" the person God wants them to be even when the physical being breaks down. Jesus said, "I have come that they may have life, and that they may have it more abundantly" (John 10:10). If it is well with the soul, it should be well in the outward man too. I pray that pastors and leaders rise up and accept, rather than reject, the older members of the church.

Someone has said that in a normal lifetime people spend 12% of their lives as children (0-12), 8% of their lives as youth (12-18), and 74% of their lives as adults (18, and up). In fact, the fastest growing segment of our population is with those who are 85 years

and up. The importance of these figures is this: typically, ministries are inversely proportional to these figures with a great effort being directed to the 8% and 12%, and the 74% are greatly neglected and downplayed as important.

Every seven seconds another American turns fifty years old. Parenting usually ends somewhere around age fifty with the empty nest; and one's career ends for at least half of the over fifty population somewhere between age fifty-seven to fifty-eight. Biologists are saying that as we learn to control pestilences and find cures for disease, humans could live for one hundred and twenty years, or more. It is a fact that more and more people are living longer; most likely you are among them. Most people who are approaching retirement can expect ten…fifteen…twenty…thirty or more years of active life. In 2006, baby boomers started to turn sixty years old at the rate of 8,000 a day, or 330 people per hour. The average life expectancy of people who turn sixty is 81.6 years, according to the U.S. Centers for Disease Control and Prevention.[17] Therefore, when believers reach forty years old, it is not time to start down the slippery slope looking forward to a life of leisure after retirement.

> Therefore, forty to fifty years old is not the time to "go over the hill" it is the time to "wind the clock" and climb to greater heights of service for the Lord.

For the Christian, older age isn't the enemy; it is simply a mile marker, reminding each one that the heavenly home is getting closer and there is a need to redeem the time (Ephesians 5: 15–16). Therefore, forty to fifty years old is not the time to "go over the hill" it is the time to "wind the clock" and climb to greater heights of service for the Lord. It's time to help the fifty plus aged adults realize that they are to set examples and be image bearers as well as seek God's purpose and calling in a greater way. They should begin to free themselves up, as "empty-nesters" gaining more discretionary time and funds to begin to make a difference in their church, their denomination, and their world. Life should get better as the years pass by. What a joy to be so loved and appreciated that they are able to sing the words of the hymn *Sweeter As the Years Go By*—and mean it!

Somewhere I once heard the quote, "The older the violin, the sweeter the tune." The church needs to be the "bow" that helps those in *the second half* to play some music that is encouraged and not rejected. Their melody should actually be accepted in a way that helps give meaning and purpose to life.

Reflect and Grow

- *If you could select any song to represent your life today, what would it be? Why?*
- *Think about your parents or older members of your church. Which songs would they select for themselves?*

- *Define ageism in your own words. Do you think ageism is more of a problem today than it was fifty years ago? Explain your response.*
- *Which scripture verses provide the most direction in dealing with the aging process personally and professionally?*

Chapter Four

Reconnect

When someone told the eighty-nine-year-old poet, Dorothy Duncan, that she had lived a "full life" she replied sharply, "Don't you dare past tense me!"

> There are many studies and many statistics to indicate rapid growth within the senior population but there is also great evidence showing that the quality of life and senior care is deteriorating even faster.

It is all too often true that the older adults in many evangelical churches may *feel* like they *are*, disconnected. It is a time to be reconnected!

Jesus said, "Behold, I say to you, lift up your eyes and look at the fields, for they are already white for harvest" (John 4:35b), and then, "The harvest truly is plentiful, but the laborers *are* few. Therefore pray the Lord of the harvest to send out laborers into His harvest" (Matthew 9:37-38). There is a harvest-field in our communities that is, "out of sight—out of mind!" There are many studies and many statistics to indicate rapid growth within the senior population but there is also great evidence showing that the quality of life and senior care is deteriorating even faster. The adult population aged sixty-five years or older, number 35.3 million and

represent approximately thirteen percent of the U.S. population. That is one of every eight Americans. This demographic is expected to double over the next three decades: that is 39.7 million by 2010; 53.7 million in 2020; and, close to 73.3 million by 2030 when the last of the Baby Boomer generation reaches legal retirement age.

At that point in time, adults in the sixty-five plus population could number one out of every five Americans. "One recent study showed that the younger a person is, the less likely he/she is to engage in religious behavior. They found that 34% of the Baby Busters [those born between 1966-1983] say they are "absolutely committed to the Christian faith," compared to 52% of Baby Boomers [those born between 1946-1964], 53% of Builders [born between 1928-1944] and 70% of Seniors [born before 1927]."[18]

An Appetite for More

Several years ago I was asked to speak at an older adult luncheon in one of our denomination churches. I was surprised and blessed to find at that event the woman from whom I had rented a room during my seminary education. I had not seen her for twenty years and she began to tell me her story. She recounted how the seminary students, to whom she rented rooms, had tried for several years to introduce her to a personal relationship with Jesus Christ. It was to no avail, and she remembered that I had told her that my youth group was praying for her salvation. She finally, along with her husband, came to Christ during the Billy Graham meetings in Boston in the summer of 1974 (the year I received my degree). She remembered that I had told her that I would pray for her, and that it would be important for her to read her Bible and get involved in an evangelical church.

"During the first eight years," she said, "I did not read the Bible, but kept remembering your words to me. Eventually, I started to read the Bible, joined a Bible study group, and became so excited about the Bible that I started my own Bible study group and have been teaching the Bible ever since." She went on to say that I was right in what I had told her, and that she really needed to get connected to the church in order to grow in her relationship with Christ. At that time she was attending this group of older adults, who had a once-a-month outreach luncheon and thoroughly enjoyed the fellowship and the good time. What a blessing to learn that she had been reconnected to the church. Her life had been changed and she was growing into the woman that God wanted her to be. As a church, we can't lose sight of this tremendous harvest field—[white (or gray) unto harvest.]

Let me mention, again, another Harvest Field! Think of the almost two million nursing home residents who live in our neighborhoods or communities. About two-thirds of those residents go into eternity each year and it is a mission field to which the church gives little thought, attention and prayer. Think of it: these residents are living at *the bridge of eternal significance.* Many in those nursing homes have become "dis-connected" from the church, but desperately need to be reconnected! We raise up missionaries and funds to send them to the *un-reached people groups,* or the *hidden people* of the world. Most of those are located in what we call the 10-40 Window. (This includes those peoples living between 10 and 40 degrees longitude of the globe.)

Yet, when we walk out of the door of our house each morning, we step into the 40-50 window where forty percent of our population is fifty years or older, and of that group 1.8 million people live in the nursing homes of America. They are a "hidden people group in plain view" of almost every church in America, and a mission field

made up of those closest to the door of eternity. This group is made up of those with an average age of 83 to 85 years, and statistics would say that a high percentage have no living relatives, receive no mail, and no visits. This mission field is virtually ignored which allows many people to die and enter a Christ-less eternity!

They Want the Main Man

As far as church visitation goes, it is not enough to send someone from the visitation committee to visit a church member. My experience tells me that the residents of this generation want to see their pastor. If the clergy fail to come, the feeling is—"My church does not care about me anymore!"

This proved true with a resident at the retirement community I served as Chaplain. He said that he did not care about making the effort to go to his own church anymore, because in the eight years that he had lived in our retirement center the pastor had not called in person or on the phone even once. He joined our worship team of volunteers and became head usher, where he found purpose and value that he no longer felt in his home church.

I have already mentioned this in passing, but take note! In the United States a person turns fifty years old every seven seconds. The Baby Boom is upon us…a tsunami of sorts, bringing in what could well be the largest wave of an un-churched population to challenge the church for years to come. As noted earlier, in 2040 those sixty-five-year olds (and above), could account for one in every four persons in our population.

Many of the Baby Boomers dropped out of the church during the cultural revolution of the 60's and 70's, never to return. It is time for those over fifty to be reconnected to God through Christ.

If they have not made a commitment that assures them of eternity with God in heaven, the *bridge of eternal significance* will forever take away their freedom of choice. Never will they have the opportunity to make any choices or changes again!

They are now in their peak earning years and are able to feed their self-consuming, self-absorbed, self-indulged tendencies. They may have an optimistic and positive attitude about the future. They figure they can accomplish anything that they want, and for the most part they even approach spirituality by their own design, in quite a secular way.

One magazine article caught my attention with the following statement.

"In a few more years when baby boomers find their way into long term care, the forms of providing spiritual care will be different from today's. Many boomers have selected a secular approach to spirituality. Rather than using traditional Western religion, many boomers will be using therapy, practice stress reduction exercises, and be involved with self-help exercises or programs to: feel better about themselves, solve their problems, and 'get their act together.' Others have found answers in the quest for beauty, art, literature, nature, physical exercise, and Eastern and other religions. Spiritual care will need to meet boomers where they are, spiritually, and assist them with the developmental tasks of aging with the resources they bring. This will likely involve offering not only the traditional kinds of religious programs found today, but also additional spiritual programs of non-religious format, such as travel and cultural opportunities, fitness programs, superior living environments, and programs that challenge them to alternative ways of thinking and living."[19]

Providing "spiritual programs of non-religious format" as stated above seems like a contradiction of terms. Meeting the basic spiritual needs of people without the spiritual services of worship, religious rituals, study of the Bible, seems quite uncomfortable to think about, but indicates the fact that spiritual well-being, defined in a broad sense, can reflect needs of mankind that are met in a purely humanistic way. Many a humanist today focuses upon the "earthy side of man" and forgets the fact that God not only created man from the dust of the earth (earthy), but set him apart from all other animals created from the dust, as He breathed into man the breath of life.

Spirituality Begins with God *Not* Man!

> The challenge is in letting people know that God is seeking to draw them to Himself through Christ Jesus and the Word as the way to deal with the deepest spiritual needs of mankind.

The challenge is in letting people know that God is seeking to draw them to Himself through Christ Jesus and the Word as the way to deal with the deepest spiritual needs of mankind. The evangelical church somehow needs to create a hunger and a thirst for that which will meet the deepest needs in an everlasting way–a relationship with Jesus Christ. Different from the upcoming baby-boomer generation, the older adults of today were part of a generation, fifty to sixty years ago, that was well aware of church membership and in a good many cases, it was a social compulsion rather than a free choice. Peter Drucker, in his Foreword to the book, *Halftime,* by Bob Buford writes:

"When I first came to this country in the '30s as an American correspondent for a group of British papers, church attendance was mandatory. The application for a mortgage that we filled out within a few weeks of our moving to this country—and in an affluent and hardly "religious" New York City suburb to boot—asked for two references, one of whom had to be the pastor of the church you attended. If you had no such reference, you could not get a mortgage. Even twenty-five years later, in the early '50s, in small town and in rural America, somebody who did not go to church did not get a bank loan or a decent job."[20]

Many of today's boomers will be unchurched, but will have been dealing with spirituality in different ways, often dabbling in Eastern religions and New Age type of expressions. Most of today's older adults at least feel that they should be at church on Sunday, though they may not have much involvement in other religious activities during the rest of the week. Boomers will satisfy their desires by buying their cars, houses and retirement homes. They'll pay their exorbitant fees for the health clubs, join country clubs and traveling clubs for seeing more of this world, pay with credit and do anything to help them *live forever.* However, unless the church purposes to reach this growing segment of the population, their design for spirituality will be insufficient on the other side of *the bridge to eternal significance.*

It may be true that older adults are not respected as God intended from the time of creation, and that they may even feel rejected by the church. However, it is now time for the church to reconnect with them and a growing boomer population.

> **None of us are here by *accident* but by the choosing of God for His purposes.**

None of us are here by *accident* but by the choosing of God for His purposes. "For by him were all things created... *all things were*

created by him, and for him (Colossians 1:16, Italics mine). Isaiah 43:7 gives man's purpose as God meant it: "Everyone who is called by My name, Whom I have created for My glory; I have formed him, yes, I have made him."

Man was created as the highest of God's creation and became a living soul when God breathed life into his nostrils and gave man a unique status in God's sight. This is what set man apart from the animal world and gave him that unique relationship with the living God. Jesus taught that man's soul was his most precious possession and that it would be a tragic thing to gain everything else and loose the soul, in reference to an eternal relationship with God (Matthew 16:26). Man was given the purpose to live for the glory of God (Ephesians 1:11-12), and when all is said and done, we are to live for God's pleasure alone. According to Revelation 4:11 (ESV), "Worthy are you, our Lord and God, to receive glory and honor and power, for you created all things, and by your will they existed and were created."

Reconnecting the Honor and Glory

> The role of the church, in relation to older adults, is to reconnect men and women with His purpose: to help them live a life that gives glory to God.

The role of the church, in relation to older adults, is to reconnect men and women with His purpose: to live a life that gives glory to God. We want to be sure that they will be "in glory" when they die. During the second half of life—this cannot be neglected as time begins to run out!

It is my observation that mainline Protestant churches have many older adults in their membership. Due to a concern to meet

their needs and care for them, these denominations seem to be the ones who have done the best job, over the years, in studying the needs and producing the resources for older adult ministry in the local church.

Evangelicals, for the most part, have been caught up in the planting of new churches and developing ministries to and for young adults and families, and have not paid much attention to older adults in their churches or their communities. They have been virtually excluded in ministry. In recent years, there seems to be a greater awareness of the need to reach out to the rapidly growing senior population, but few are meeting those needs. In a few years they will weight the scales of the population to the older side of the age bracket. Unfortunately few denominations are adequately addressing this demographic. This is confirmed in an article titled Ministry to Senior Adults on the National Association of Evangelicals website dated January 1, 1998 | RESOLUTION. Here is the quote: "The senior adult population in the United States of America is growing three times more rapidly than the national population rate. In spite of this fact, only 1% of the churches surveyed have a director of adult ministry, while 80% of the same churches have a volunteer or paid youth worker. Senior adults possess the capacity to grow spiritually and enrich the lives of others. Too few churches provide real resources for spiritual growth or provide senior adult ministries beyond recreational activities." (https://www.nae.org/ministry-to-senior-adults/) I don't know the statistics today, but I would guess that this is still pretty much the same. There are many churches around the country that do have, perhaps, a monthly luncheon for seniors, or a Sunday School Class, and hopefully someone on staff that visits the homebound, but this is often a segment of the church culture that is neglected. I am aware of two denominations that have specific ministry to Senior

Adults. The Covenant Church of America has a ministry called Crescendo, and the other is called the Senior Adult Ministry of the Assemblies of God.

However, there are other groups that are stepping up to fill in where the church falls short. Some of the para-church groups I know about include Christ Above Politics, formerly The Christian Association of Prime Timers (Christian Alternative to AARP), The Community Chaplain Service, God Cares Ministry, Spiritual Eldercare, (Nursing Home Ministry Resources), Halftime, Significant Living Travel, Mission Next, formerly The Finisher's Project, Elder Care and Links, a collection of older adult resources sent out periodically by Tom McCormick. The Upper Room Ministry has an Older Adult section on the website with books and devotionals, and Senior Living Ministries produces a daily devotional, Monday through Friday as well as blog posts. A website titled The Oldst Ministry Paradigm lists a number of books directed toward Older Adults and Older Adult Ministries. For Grandparents wanting to have purposeful ministry to their adult children and grandchildren there are two wonderful ministries with resources focusing on Intentional Christian Grandparenting. The oldest being The Christian Grandparenting Network, founded by Cavin Harper about twenty-four years ago, and a more recent ministry named The Legacy Coalition founded in 2016. Also a related ministry to the Christian Grandparenting Network is Elderquest: Engaging the Generations Founded by the Executive Director, Cavin Harper, and Grandparents N' Charge, Founder and President, Gloria Williams.

Each year a few more books are being published on the subject and it seems that there are ample resources being provided for the development of evangelical ministry to older adults. It is imperative that evangelical seminaries, in the preparation of future ministers,

begin to include more emphasis on older adult ministry in the curriculum.

Ministries for those in the fifty plus age group need to be redesigned keeping Him in mind—not the senior and not the church. We need to help this population group live their second half for eternal significance but it won't be accomplished with social gatherings.

What do the Scriptures tell us about the purpose and goals for older adults who are either a part of our churches or needing to be reached in our communities? For the Christian older adult the fifty plus years should be filled with fruitfulness and purpose: "Those who are planted in the house of the LORD shall flourish in the courts of our God. They shall still bear fruit in old age; they shall be fresh and flourishing…" (Psalm 92:13 –14). The psalmist gives a wonderful purpose statement for the second half, no matter what the age; "Now also when I am old and gray headed, O God, do not forsake me, until I declare Your strength to this generation, Your power to everyone *who* is to come" (Psalm 71:18).

Today's youth have very few heroes upon which to build their lives. Just think of the wonderful purpose and opportunity to contribute to the lives of grandchildren, great-grandchildren and youth in the churches. Perhaps our churches could begin to open up generational connections through joint Sunday school classes, older adult/youth outings from time to time, or adopt-a-grandparent programs. Older adults could read to children, or listen to "memory verses" at the children's programs during the week.

A couple of years ago, I was in a seminar on post-modernism and one of the participants, a young woman in her twenties, made

an interesting comment. She said that her generation, known as the Gen-Xer's, was a generation of young people that did not have much to hold on to in their lives, coming from broken families, and all in all, were kind of lost in society. What if the Gen-Xer's could make a list of questions they want answered. Wouldn't the list look something like this?

- *How can we have a good marriage?*
- *How did you balance a career and marriage?*
- *How did you keep a personal relationship with Jesus alive and balance a career and marriage?*
- *How can we parent with healthy, holy and whole relationships rooted in biblical truths?*

They would have a desire to learn from these older adults, and yet they feel repelled by them. The older generation isn't quite sure what to do about their colored hair, pierced body parts, etc. Yet this younger generation would like to draw upon the wisdom that seems to have given these older adults a secure and sure foundation to living.

She said that she felt like her generation was a threat to these older adults with whom they desperately wanted a relationship. The very thing that the younger generation wants is standing in the way of meaningful relationships. Two-way communication is vitally important for both age groups.

Reflect and Grow

- *In addition to creating a hunger and thirst in the over-fifty-group, how can the church keep them fed and watered?*
- *What can the church do to rise up heroes in all generations?*
- *Regarding inter-generational communication, how comfortable*

are the leaders or your church or community in getting different age groups to share ideas, activities and concerns?

Chapter Five

Winding the Clock—Redeeming the Time

If adults are to accomplish fruit-bearing in their older adult years, they will need to look at things differently. Rather than forty years old being *over the hill,* instead I would like to suggest that it is time to wind the clock. Older generations would understand the analogy of a wind up clock, whereas the younger ones would most likely only know about clocks that use batteries or are found in their cell phones, I Phones, I Pads, etc.

As a windup clock slows down and stops until wound up again, the mid-life adult needs to take the clock key of their life and wind it up so that it will keep going. At forty years old there is a need to begin winding…preparing for the future…as a person looks forward to being free of work and other responsibilities and to prepare for the most effective years of service for the Lord. One day the clock will stop never to be wound up again!

It might be pictured as in the illustration below.

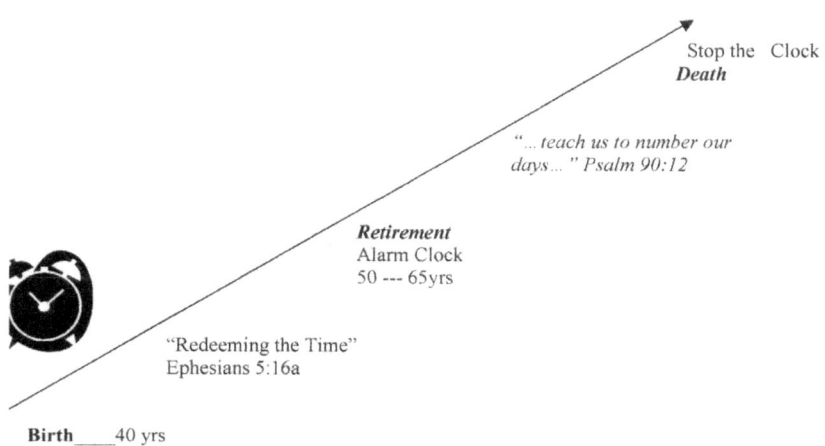

Stop the Clock
Death

"... teach us to number our days... " Psalm 90:12

Retirement
Alarm Clock
50 --- 65yrs

"Redeeming the Time"
Ephesians 5:16a

Birth_____40 yrs

"Winding the Clock—Redeeming the Time"

From my earliest days of ministry with older adults beginning in 1976, I have built my ministry upon the foundation of the lives of two godly adults found in Luke 2. Their names were Simeon and Anna. My vision for ministry developed from the insight that I believe God gave to me, in those early years, as I read about these two people who found their purpose in life, and death, in a relationship with Jesus Christ.

The mission is built upon two goals. *First,* introduce salvation through Christ Jesus alone. Simeon had the promise from God that he would not see death until he had seen Christ (Luke 2:26). It is important for older adults to find, and then grow in a relationship with God through Jesus so that they will have assurance that they can die in peace and be assured of heaven (2:29-30). *Second,* offer opportunities for service. Anna, who had been a widow for eighty-four years, had spent those years serving God with fasting and prayer, night and day in the temple (2:37). Anna's life is an example

> **When people begin to prioritize *before* they begin to have more discretionary time and money, they can better use those future years for eternal significance.**

of one who served the Lord and put Him first.

Once this second-half generation has established a relationship with the Lord, they need to be encouraged to grow in worship and service for the Lord. In order for that to happen, there is the need to do some planning, and there is no better time to do that than before they enter *the second half of life* after fifty years old. Somewhere between the years of forty and forty-five, it is time to *wind the clock;* and with each turn of the knob think about the issues; financial, health related, prevention, housing, spiritual growth, spiritual giftedness and how God could use them in the future. Perhaps these are the most effective years of ministry-related service as they have more freedom in time and finances.

When people begin to prioritize *before* they begin to have more discretionary time and money, they can better use those future years for eternal significance. Thoughts should begin to center on *calling and purpose* rather than career. Howard Hendricks made this statement in a message that I heard at a conference for older adults; "Our occupation is what we are *paid for*, but our vocation (*calling*) is what we are *made for*."[21]

In view of the increasing numbers of the over-fifty aged adults in society and in our churches, there will be a greater opportunity for churches to develop ministries to reach those who do not know Christ and release those who do for service to the Lord. Some may develop ministries designed to bring hope, spiritual growth, more intergenerational interdependence, a deeper involvement of mutual help and fellowship among older adults, and help to make

the second half years more meaningful years. As long as God gives life, believers are called to glorify God, according to Ephesians 1:12, "that we who first trusted in Christ should be to the praise of His glory." Paul reminded the listeners on Mars Hill, "In Him we live and move and have our being" (Acts 17:28). Colossians 3:17 reminds each older believer, "And whatever you do in word or deed, *do* all in the name of the Lord Jesus, giving thanks to God the Father through Him."

A woman who served on the coordinating committee for older adult ministry in our local, district ministry came to a meeting one day and said, "This is my last meeting!" She had served from the beginning of this ministry and now, at ninety-two years old felt called to something greater. She said, "I have been driving ladies from the community to appointments, have had many opportunities to share my faith, and I need to give more time to 'my ladies'. They are *my church!*" I don't want to miss the opportunities that God is giving me. I don't know how much time I, or they, have left and I believe that God had brought these ladies to me."

To Practice the Presence of Christ—Just "Be"

What if the older adult can't "do" anymore? After the *can't do* realization settles in, then the *be* plays an important role. Read what Paul has to say in 2 Corinthians 4:16. These words do not give an attractive picture of aging, but does give a wonderful promise "Therefore we do not lose heart. Even though our outer man is perishing (NIV, 'wasting away'), yet the inward man is being renewed day by day."

I remember Carl's body was shutting down due to the ills of cancer. He could not "do" anymore, like he had done before as a successful businessman and servant of the Lord, but as he laid in his bed his godly heart allowed him to simply practice the presence of Christ—to "be" the person God wanted him to be. What a ministry he had to others! I visited him a few days before his death. After a short visit that included the reading of Scripture and prayer, he said to me as I was leaving the room, "Please come back! I'm embarrassed," he said, "You prayed for me and I didn't even offer to pray for you. How can I pray for you and your family?"

I returned, and this man, whose body was wasting away— ministered the presence of Christ, through prayer, as he simply sought to "be" the person that

> Older adults who spend time in God's Word, handle crisis, changes and challenges of aging with a greater strength than those who do not make time for the Word of God.

he believed God wanted him to be even as he struggled with this illness that soon took him to heaven. He knew that his body would soon return to dust, but he was ready to die. He had put his faith in God through Jesus Christ many years before, and wanted to use his dying days to *connect* his visitors to God through prayer, if by no other means.

Peter says that we ought to "grow in the grace and knowledge of our Lord and Savior Jesus Christ" (2 Peter 3:18). For that to happen we must rely upon the Word of God to instruct us with words such as these, "So then faith comes by hearing, and hearing by the word of God" (Romans 10:17). It has been my observation that Christian older adults who spend time in God's Word, handle

the crisis, changes and challenges of aging with a greater strength than those who do not make time for the Word of God.

One resident stopped me often to say she liked my story about the boy who told his father that he knew what the word Bible means. The son told his dad, "It's simple. B-I-B-L-E…Basic Information Before Leaving Earth." A nurse one day came to me and said, "Do you know why people should read their Bible's more as they get older?" The answer is *to study for the final exams!* Romans 10:17 came to mean much to me as I ministered to residents and saw the benefit of a strong, growing faith that is built upon the Scriptures.

Fight and Finish with Faith

When we come to the end of our lives we want to be able to know that we finished well, as Paul said in what many have called his final words, "For I am already being poured out as a drink offering, and the time of my departure is at hand. I have fought the good fight, I have finished the race, I have kept the faith" (2 Tim. 4:6-8).

The psalmist writes, "So teach us to number our days, that we may gain a heart for wisdom" (Psalm 90:12). It is believed that Moses wrote this psalm; perhaps as he was about to finish his long life of service to God. He had lived 120 years, and yet he wrote that the normal lifespan would be seventy to eighty years. Looking back over his life, he spent his first forty years in Egypt preparing to take leadership of bringing God's people through the wilderness to the Promised Land. His actual years of service to God were about eighty years. Perhaps this was in his mind as he penned these words about numbering our days. He also wrote, "Oh, that they were wise, that they understood this, that they would consider their latter end" (Deuteronomy 32:39).

A person with a seventy-year life span has about 18,000 days of potentially useful service for the Lord, assuming that his first twenty or so years are spent in education and training. It is not so important that we count our days, but make our days count,

> As long as they can serve Him, they ought to do so, and when they have reached a point when they are no longer able to *actively* serve, then they need to *be* the person God wants them to be and have a testimony that continues until death.

and count for the Lord. As older adults "number their days" it is important that they are growing in the Lord, so that they continue to "grow in grace, and in the knowledge of our Lord and Savior Jesus Christ" (2 Peter 3:18). John DeBrine of the radio program called *Songtime,* which I listened to for many years, often said, "Grow in grace so you won't groan in disgrace."

Older Adults Need Purpose!

That purpose ought to be one that is honoring to the Lord. As long as they can serve Him, they ought to do so, and when they have reached a point when they are no longer able to *actively* serve, then they need to *be* the person God wants them to be and have a testimony that continues until death. It is unfortunate that some of the older adults who have been in the church *all* their lives, are not growing and seem to be weak in their faith.

I read a story some time ago about a boy who fell out of his bed as he slept. His mother asked him, "Why did you fall out of bed?" The answer was simple but true. He said, "I guess it was because I stayed too close to the getting-in place."

The apostle Paul writes, "Brethren, do not be children in understanding; however, in malice be babes, but in understanding be mature" (1 Corinthians 14:20). It is dishonoring to the Lord to remain as spiritual children. We need to have the faith of a little child according to God's Word. In other words, just a simple trust, and yet, in our understanding we must grow up, always going forward in our faith.

The challenge to those who are leaders of older adult groups in the church, as well as that of the chaplain who is ministering in a continuing care retirement center or nursing home, is to keep the people moving forward with a growing faith. For some this means entering a saving relationship with God through Jesus Christ for the very first time in their lives. For those who made an early decision in life, it may be just challenging them to look back at that decision, become more purposeful, and continue to grow in their faith.

At a special series of meetings during the Lenten season a couple of years ago, a woman came to me at the end of the evening and said that she had raised her hand to recommit her life to Christ. At the age of twelve in confirmation class she had made her initial decision, but had not paid too much attention to it through the years.

On another occasion, a resident came to my office on Tuesday following the previous Sunday worship service, with the bulletin insert that he had signed. The insert was a statement of commitment for salvation or recommitment to Christ. This physician said that it had reminded him of a commitment that he had made in his confirmation class when he was about twelve years old, and thought it was good that he recommit himself to Christ.

Another woman, who had been a church organist for fifty years in a mainline protestant church, faithfully attended our weekly Bible studies. She had many emotional needs and was extremely fragile mentally when she entered our retirement home. In fact, so fragile that she quickly fell apart emotionally and physically at the slightest challenge or fear. About two days after her return to her room from a floor that offered more medical care the entire facility was quarantined. This was due to an upper respiratory syndrome spreading rapidly throughout the healthcare center. She became so fretful that she had to be placed in the psychiatric hospital as a result of her fear of becoming ill.

Sometime later, after returning to our facility, she came to me after a weekly Bible study that she had regularly attended and said, "I often hear you mention being born-again and want to know exactly what you mean." I had the privilege of leading her to a "new-birth" salvation experience that day! Quite appropriately the altar of that important decision was the piano bench in our chapel. She had spent many years ministering and leading people in worship at the piano and organ. That afternoon, at the piano in our chapel, she prayed to receive Christ into her life by asking Him to forgive her sin and to come into her life as her personal Savior.

Her life changed! She established close friendships with residents who later died but found a new strength to go on through those losses. She also had a bout with breast cancer and also fractured both hips. She handled these physical and emotional setbacks with an amazing inner strength that was lacking when she first arrived at our home. In a staff meeting, her name came up and some nurses who had been in employment long enough to remember her fragile spirit said, "Elim Park has been good for her!" One nurse continued, "I don't know what has happened, but she has gained so much emotional strength." I knew the real answer. It was an inner

strengthening from the Holy Spirit and the presence of Christ in her life. Not only had she come to meet Jesus as her Savior but also had been nurtured through personal relationships with strong, mature believers and was able to establish friendships through the years.

The last of those meaningful relationships was with a retired pastor. Weekly Bible study was also an important priority in her life. She found new purpose for living and the result was a personal strength and a serving spirit that was of benefit to a number of residents through the years. She was reconnected to the Lord, whom she had served through the years, but never had come to know in a personal way.

A New Outlet

I think of another lady, Esther, who described herself as an agnostic college professor throughout her life. Though she had been retired for many years, and eventually moved into our retirement community, she was an avid reader and a *lifetime student*. She developed a wonderful relationship with a resident who had been a pastor, and was now well into his retirement years. As a result of that relationship, she became a born-again believer and became so excited about her faith that she used every spare moment to study the Scriptures. She wasted no time in making up for lost years as she wished that she had come to know Jesus Christ earlier in her life. She decided that she would invest the rest of her life on earth learning as much as she could about God's Word and her new friend, Jesus Christ.

Near the end, she spoke at our morning devotions and used her copious notes that she kept as she studied. After her death, I was blessed when her family decided to give those study notes to me.

(I was also given many of the written sermons, radio messages, and funeral services of the pastor who led her to Christ.) These "growing believers" were a blessing and left a wonderful and meaningful heritage to me in the last years of their lives, as they "bore fruit in old age" (Psalm 92:13–14). And it was the result of being reconnected.

"Faith, far from turning us away from the world, brings us back to it," says Paul Tournier in his book, *The Adventure of Living*. He says, "Faith awakens in us a new interest in the world, in the concrete reality of every day, and no matter how hard and difficult or painful it is, it is wonderful at the same time. The joy of living, often realized in the simple things of life, brings great pleasure. The joy of feeling that what we do is absolutely unique, that no one else will ever be who we are, that no other moment in life will ever be the same as the present one, that the joy of each experience, each act, each success, is what it means to be made in God's image, is the very thing that should give us the courage to live."[22]

Shedding Things

He goes on to remind us, "There are disappointments, snags and failures. Even our successes are never either final or complete. He says that the older one becomes the tally of abandoned projects and hopes increase. There is the realization that some things will never be accomplished with the diminishing capacity of work and its declining faculties. Does that mean the adventure is over? Absolutely not!" He continues on to share, "Adventure goes only one way: always forward. If old age is only backward looking, whether in pride or in sorrow, it is going to run against the current of life. Every age has it's own adventure. And sooner or later, suddenly or gradually, everything will end in death." Tournier goes on to say, "The past is but a training ground for adventure. A man's

lifework is his life, so therefore, old age can still be turned toward the future; yes, all the way to death!"

Jesus Christ made a success of his life by being "obedient unto death" (Philippians 2:8). The meaning of life is to live in obedience to God. Tournier says that, "in detaching himself from

> "A man's lifework is his life, so therefore, old age can still be turned toward the future; yes, all the way to death!"
>
> -   Tournier

particular things and ephemeral actions, and attaching himself instead to transcendent values, in accepting his human condition, necessarily fragile, temporary, limited, and incomplete, the aged person is still obeying God, who made men "strangers and exiles on earth" (Hebrews 11:13). From the cradle, onward, life is a choice; a choice of shedding things throughout the stages of life until there is a revision of values that must take place in the later years of life. It is as if we are pouring all the multiple things of life into a funnel until the things that are of utmost importance remain. Old age is filled with losses, but if Christ is a part of our life, we realize that when everything else is taken away, Jesus says, "I will never leave you, nor forsake you" (Hebrews 13:5)."

As we age, we experience many losses. It is more and more important to find strength from a faith that is growing strong as the losses continue to multiply as the years pass by. The other side of spiritual multiplication (gain rather than loss) is stated in Peter's salutation recorded in 2 Peter 1:2-3a (KJV). "Grace and peace be multiplied unto you through the knowledge of God, and of Jesus our Lord, according to his divine power..." Here is the answer to gaining strength in the onslaught of losses: the knowledge of

God that comes through a relationship with Jesus Christ and yields power to go on.

The Apostle Paul's words confirm this, "But we have this treasure in earthen vessels, that the excellence of the power may be of God and not of us. *We are* hard-pressed on every side, yet not crushed; *we are* perplexed, but not in despair; persecuted, but not forsaken; struck down, but not destroyed, always carrying about in the body the dying of the Lord Jesus, that the life of Jesus also may be manifested in our body" (2 Corinthians 4:7-10). Paul goes on to describe what is known in the physical world as the law of entropy, the fact that over time things self-destruct and diminish. A few years ago our family cleaned my grandmother's house after her death. We found that the aged cloth, metal, wood, and paper seemed to become ragged, rusted, rotted, and disintegrated over time and had no worth but to be thrown out to the rubbish heap. I could not help but be reminded that for human beings it is the same; the body is destroyed bit by bit until it is ready for burial in the ground. Yet for the believer in Christ, Paul says that, "... Even though our outward man is perishing, yet the inward *man* is being renewed day by day" (2 Corinthians 4:16). A couple of verses later it says, "We do not look at the things which are seen, but at the things which *are* not seen. For the things which are seen *are* temporary, but the things which are not seen are eternal" (vs.18). Life's purpose is to find God's purpose and prepare to meet Him at death. This can only be accomplished through faith in Jesus Christ.

Our world gives more value to the visible than the invisible. And this is a message that is not very favorable to old age, and, as a result, causes the aged to feel devalued and ill at ease. Often they feel useless and rejected, because, as Tournier puts it, "The adventure of life is defined only as action." Yet, he emphasizes, "the greatest of adventure is not action, but our own development." As

long as a person in the older years can "do" it does involve action. But when that person can no longer "do" there is a much-increased dependence upon God and a decreased dependence on men and the world for inner development.

The words of Jesus remind the older adult (as well as any person at any age) that he who loses his life for Jesus accepts a new adventure of the revision of values, and is prepared to let go of all the treasures accumulated on earth, in order to grab on to Christ for all eternity. "For whoever desires to save his life will lose it, but whoever loses his life for My sake will find it. For what profit is it to a man if he gains the whole world, and loses his own soul? Or what will a man give in exchange for his soul" (Matthew 16:25–26)? The note in *The Defender's Study Bible* says, "This is a remarkable profit and loss statement! The Greek word for "soul" is psuche, from which we have our English word "psychology," meaning "study of the soul." Although it can also mean "life," depending on the context, the emphasis and comparison here seems clearly to refer to one's eternal soul."[23]

Yes, the physical body may die, bit by bit, but the soul has "life," and that is the part that can be renewed day by day. In Agenda, the newsletter of the Presbyterian Older Adult Ministry Network is an article titled, *The Soul-making Years,* which states, "Carl G. Jung's psychology calls for a different orientation in old age. For Jung, the early years are the time for ego development, but the second half of life is for the full development of the Self. The Self is the unique image of God that each of us is." He says, "We must get beyond the place of equating ourselves with ego or past accomplishments and always reach within ourselves for more strength and outside of ourselves to grow and change."[24] The article says that it is a time for *soul-making,* a time for the *flowering of the personality.*

When a person comes to know Christ as Savior in youth or in old age, his life begins to blossom. In the older years the flower begins to unfold and through growth spiritually should produce a beautiful flower that is a sweet- smelling savor to the Lord and a wonderful testimony to others of the beauty of Christ (2 Corinthians 2:15). The word picture in the last sentence reminds me of a banner that hung in the chapel of a nursing home that I used to visit in New Bedford, Massachusetts. It said, "Bloom Where You Are Planted." In other words, live for the glory of God, and serve Him wherever you are in your life and your abilities.

W. Glyn Evans shared in a devotional, "This is what you did for me, Lord, when I first heard Your name and gave my heart to You. The barren wilderness became green as the water of life started to trickle through my life (Psalm 107:35)."[25] Fruit and flowers began to grow, and people began to notice and comment on them. That was the delightful life, and it still is when Your water makes my life green and beautiful." Evans concludes, "If I stay myself continually upon Him, He will multiply the little I have. My barrenness will give way to fertile fields." [26]

As people are living longer and face the ever-growing longevity issue, there will be a greater opportunity to explore what might be called "soul work." In the work of Dr. Lars Tornstam, a new concept called *geretranscendence* is regarded as the final stage when the individual becomes less self-occupied, and at the same time more selective in the choice of social and other activities. The individual may also experience a decrease of interest in material things and find a greater need for solitary "meditation," or positive solitude, that becomes more important. Many older adults have spent quality time reading the Bible, individually, or involved in a group Bible Study at the close of their years, with great benefit. Old age transcendence, or "living above the circumstances," is

characterized by those who "sit in heavenly places in Christ Jesus" (Ephesians 2:6). They seem to have a different view of life!

Living Above the Circumstances

I worked at a summer camp and had charge of the camp store. While setting up before camp began, I was placing greeting cards on the rack when I came across one that said, "Keep looking down." I thought this to be strange, because I was used to telling people to keep looking up! When I opened the card, it finished the sentence: "Keep looking down because you are seated in the heavenly places in Christ Jesus!" What a great reminder to the older adult who is struggling with life. The believer's position in Christ allows them to live above the circumstances. No longer should the believer say, "Well, under the circumstances, not so bad," when asked, "How are you?" The believer's position is *above!*

The only true place to find that adventure of living and abundance of life is in Jesus. The source for this contentment is outside of humanity and in God; as people come to salvation through Jesus Christ, the Holy Spirit indwells the believer and gives an inner peace, contentment, and strength. Paul says, "Yet indeed I also count all things loss for the excellence of the knowledge of Christ Jesus my Lord, for whom I have suffered the loss of all things, and count them as rubbish, that I may gain Christ" (Philippians 3:8). The Defender's Study notes say that to "win Christ" means to "be gain for Christ," and "we should not only seek to gain Christ and His salvation for ourselves, but we should also be spiritually profitable in His service."[27] In other words, as long as a person has life, he is to live for the glory of God. Tournier says, "to lose everything, and to accept it--that is indeed adventure." [28] Glyn Evans writes,

I do not like a "cross" religion...I crave a "glory" religion—a religion of feeling, fame, joy and happiness... Yet I read of Jesus, "who for the joy that was set before him endured the cross" (Hebrews 12:2). Jesus found joy in the cross, while I shun it. I do not want to bear the cross (die to self to do the will of God). If I submit, the joy of the cross will see me through many a dark day. The joy is not the cross itself, but its aftermath, for God always deals with ends—final realities—not routes to them.[29]

Again Tournier makes an important comment that this necessary detachment from the world means closer fellowship with God (perhaps this was "the joy set before Christ").

"The discovery of the world in childhood is an approach toward God through wonder at His works. The adventure of the adult is the experience of God in action--inspired and guided by Him. All through our lives we are learning to know Him; first through study, then through action, and then through adoration, and all three adventures are but one. There is always a "new God" to discover and a familiar God to rediscover, and always a forward march." [30]

The Source of Adventure

I talked to a man in the summer of 2000 who told me that he took an early retirement because he wanted to give the rest of his active years to Christ. He got involved in a program called Outward Bound in South Africa, to which he traveled twice.

He climbed Mt. Kilamajaro in his mid-seventies. When I spoke to him, again, in the late summer of 2001, he and his wife had just returned from canoeing down the Colorado River. In October, he cancelled out of a speaking engagement at a study week for older adults because he was involved with the Chuck Colson ministry

of Prison Fellowship and was traveling to Washington, DC for a special meeting of their leaders following 9/11. This man certainly

> "But the present is real, alive, active, and important; to miss God's purpose for me today, would cripple the future as well as neutralize the beneficial lessons of the past."
>
> W. Glyn Evans

was living a life of adventure; and that adventure involved not only the enjoyment of life, but also the desire to live in service to the Lord. He told me, "Since I've been retired, I've seen God work some real miracles." This man was on an adventure each day of his retirement, and believed that God was the source of that adventure that gave him great joy each day as he sought to serve Him.

Evans notes that we can live according to God's clock, which is built upon a timeless plan. In fact, he says, "Right now we are living in the present, but this present is made up of the past and we can't know how it will be built into the future." I guess my observation would be that we can only rely upon the fact that hindsight is always quite enlightening--in fact, 20/20 vision—so that we can look back and see how things have fit together. We also know that "All things work together for good to them that love God and are called according to his purposes" (Romans 8:28). "My life right now," says Evans, "is my past, because those experiences of the past have worked their way into my life for now. It is foolish to dwell on the future because I do not yet know what God has in store for me. But the present is real, alive, active, and important; to miss God's purpose for me today, would cripple the future as well as neutralize the beneficial lessons of the past." He goes on to say that "the only schedule I must keep is a *day schedule* even as was kept by Jesus, who worked 'the works of Him who sent Him as long as it was

day'" (John 9:4). He reminds the reader that God does not usually publish His schedules (except rarely) and therefore he must live by faith--and faith says, "Lord, you have your eye on my schedule and your hand on me." [31]

The Psalmist reminds us that God has ordained the number of our days before we even live one of them upon this earth (139:16) and that we simply must live one day at a time (Matthew 6:34), seeking to do God's will, and seeking to be content with the adventure. Any adventure has its struggles, as will life itself. When we "wind the clock" at midlife we look forward to the days that God will give us when we become free from work and other things that normally take up our time, so that we can use our time for Him.

> Each day, we must keep the clock wound because we know that one day the alarm will sound and it will be God's call for us to cross over from our life experience – filled with adventure – to life eternal which will be *the* greatest adventure of them all.

Each day, we must keep the clock wound because we know that one day the alarm will sound and it will be God's call for us to cross over from our life experience, filled with adventure, to life eternal which will be the greatest adventure of them all. If we have been saved from God's wrath the adventure will be filled with joy ("in Thy presence is fullness of joy," Psalm 16:11); and if not, filled with God's wrath ("and he who does not believe the Son…the wrath of God abides on him" John 3:36).

Advancing in the Adventure

How do we continue to grow in our spirituality as we advance in this adventure of life to fulfill God's purpose? It is a process that can begin at any age. If during our youth and middle age we could instill the concept of how we might create a meaningful time in our old age, we might have a higher likelihood of achieving it. It is vitally important that the Word of God becomes an integral part of our lives in the early years. When those words are written upon our hearts and became the basis of every activity and decision of life, as older adults we will have a stronger faith to journey on into this adventure. John 15:10-11says, "If you keep my commandments, you will abide in my love; just as I have kept my Father's commandments, and abide in His love. These things have I spoken to you, that my joy may remain in you, and that your joy may be full." We know the reality of the abundant life as our faith is built upon God's Word.

Long life is a gift given to us by God, and it is documented as follows, "With long life I will satisfy him, and show him My salvation" (Psalm 91:16). According to His plan the average lifespan is seventy years (Psalm 90:10). In the older years, God promises, "Even to your old age I am he; and even to gray hairs will I carry you: I have made, and I will bear; even I will carry, and deliver you" (Isaiah 46:4).

Conditional and Contingent Promises

We have to do more than desire and want to have a relationship with Jesus: we have to get up out of our comfy chairs and actually do something. The promises are conditional upon a personal relationship with God through Jesus Christ. They are contingent

upon faith, and, "Faith comes by hearing, and hearing by the word of God." The Word of God is "life" to the believer.

- Genesis 2:7 - "And the LORD God formed man of the dust of the ground, and breathed into his nostrils the breath of life; and man became a living soul."
- John 6:63b - "The words that I speak to you are spirit, and they are life."
- 2 Timothy 3:15 - "All Scripture is given by inspiration of God…" The NIV translates the word "inspiration" in this verse with the word "God-breathed." The whole concept of God breathing out all (every word of) Scripture is the idea that God produced the Scripture somewhat like He did creation.
- Psalm 33:6 - "By the word of the LORD were the heavens made; and all the host of them by the breath of his mouth."

The same God that breathed breath into man so that he would become a living soul is the same God that breathed revelation to man by way of the Scripture. Revelation is the act of God whereby He imparts information, which we could not know otherwise. It is information that deals primarily with the Person, the work, and the plan of God. In 2 Peter 1:3 and 4 we read, "As His divine power has given unto us all things that pertain to life and godliness, through the knowledge of Him who called us by glory and virtue: by which have been given to us exceedingly great and precious promises: that through these you might be partakers of the divine nature...."

Through the power of the work of the Holy Spirit in the process of inspiration and illumination, those precious promises (words) nourish the soul of the believer and give direction in all matters relating to life and to our

> **Though men conveyed the words, we must remember that it was not the men that were inspired but the words.**

relationship with God. Though men conveyed the words, we must remember that it was not the men that were inspired but the words. Through inspiration, God told men what He wanted to relate and those men wrote it down. The Holy Spirit guided those men in such a way that He allowed each writer to write those words according to his own unique style and also guided them so that those words were written without error. 2 Peter 1:21 affirms, "For prophecy never came by the will of man: but holy men of God spoke as they were moved by the Holy Spirit."

One author explained it like this: "Just as when one exhales his breath, and that breath comes from his innermost being, so ultimately all scripture is to be viewed as the very product of God himself. God and his words are inseparable, which is one reason the Bible is often referred to as God's Word." [32] It seems to make sense that "the living soul"—in breathed by God can only be nourished by "the living words of God;" that is, the Scriptures. We can only gain understanding (illumination) when we establish a relationship to God with "the Living Word"–Jesus Christ.

It is only as we establish a relationship with God through the revealed and Living Word of God that we are assured of crossing over the *Bridge of Eternal Significance,* from Life Experience to Life Eternal. This is our only secure connection to God and heaven. If a person makes it to the second half of life, and has not yet been reconnected to his Father in heaven they have no assurance

of crossing from life's experience into eternity with God. This only happens if we are reconnected to God.

Sin that marred that image and broke humanity's connection with God has a simple solution; and that is simply being reconnected through the person of His Son, Jesus Christ. At that point, a person is assured of crossing that Bridge of Eternal Significance, secure in God and life everlasting in his eternal presence. The church of Jesus Christ needs to help all people find the means of reconnection. It is the only way to *finish well!*

These Things Theology

In order for a good finish, we need to focus upon what is important in our relationship with the Lord and consider leaving a legacy that is an encouragement to others. [33] (footnote has one too many a space. The aging Peter reflects upon this in his letter in the New Testament. In his youth he was bold and impetuous but in his later years he seems to have mellowed out and become quite pastoral. At the same time, he seemed to take a look at his priorities and throw everything into a funnel, allowing all but one thought to come down the narrow neck as that which is most important at the conclusion of his life. It is his legacy that is expressed in what I would call his *"these things* theology" as found in 2 Peter 1:5 – 15:

"But also for this very reason, giving all diligence, add to your faith virtue, to virtue knowledge, to knowledge self-control, to self-control perseverance, to perseverance godliness, to godliness brotherly kindness, and to brotherly kindness love. For if *these things* are yours and abound, *you will be* neither barren nor unfruitful in the knowledge of our Lord Jesus Christ. For he who *lacks these things* is shortsighted, even to blindness, and has forgotten that he was cleansed from his old sins. Therefore, brethren, be even more

87

diligent to make your call and election sure, for if you *do **these things*** you will never stumble; for so *an entrance* will be supplied *to you abundantly into the everlasting kingdom* of our Lord and Savior Jesus Christ. For this reason I will not be negligent to *remind you always of **these things***, though you know and are established in the present truth. Yes, I think it is right, as long as I am in this tent, to stir you up by reminding *you,* knowing that shortly I must put off my tent, just as our Lord Jesus Christ showed me. Moreover I will be careful to ensure that you always *have a reminder of **these things*** after my decease." (Emphasis is mine.)

"These things" are in reference to the eight character qualities that I call, Peter's Steps to Purposeful Living. (See the illustration below) The first and most important step is faith: faith in God through Jesus Christ and then a daily life that is lived by faith. Then, added to faith are the steps to purposeful living, with the result: "so that an entrance shall be ministered unto you abundantly into the everlasting kingdom of our Lord and Savior Jesus Christ" (verse 11).

"Peter's Steps to Purposeful Living"

"Abundant Entrance to Glory"

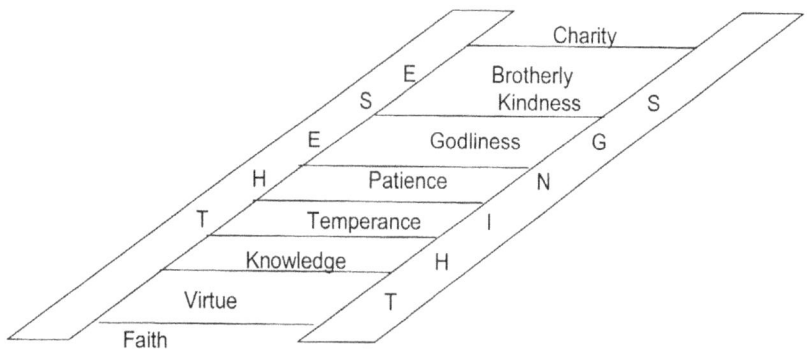

"These Things Theology"

Grady R. Henley, in a Sunday school lesson entitled *Ministering Long After We Die* says "It is interesting that in 2 Kings 13:14 we, again, find the mention of Elisha for the first time in forty-three years. He is eighty years old and dying of some lingering disease. This seems significant for two reasons. First, his mentor Elijah was taken up to heaven by a whirlwind and did not face death. The second reason is that Elisha, in his earthly ministry, had the ability to raise the dead and heal others of their diseases; yet, here he is facing his own death. There is neither whirlwind nor healing in his future, only death. Did he lack faith or was there sin in his life? No! It simply means that God had a different plan for Elisha.

The last reference to Elisha was in the events of 2 Kings 9:1 which preceded this passage by forty–three years. What was Elisha doing all those years? We don't know! But there is one thing that is

very remarkable about him, and it is this; he retained the title "the man of God" which means that he must have remained faithful in his service to God. There is no record of miracles or anything spectacular. It must mean that he was just doing routine faithful service--day in and day out, minding the things of God. The bulk of spirituality is this rather mundane faithfulness everyday. It is this everyday consistently faithful service that leaves the greatest testimony of our lives—not the occasional miracles that catch people's attention." [34]

Each person will leave a legacy, or a *life message* that will carry well after they are gone. In the producing of a *life message* each chapter should describe a more intense and close relationship with the Author of our lives. Older adults are writing the final chapters of their life message and the question is—how will the book end? Concerning Job's life we read in Job 8:7, "Though your beginning was small, yet your latter end would increase abundantly" and in chapter 42:12a, "So the Lord blessed the latter end of Job more than his beginning." If life has been rewarding—so far, a person can only look forward to a greater reward, as he is faithful to the Lord. A faithful believer looks forward to the reward of being in God's presence for all eternity, which certainly is a whole lot better than earthly life.

If a person is to leave a remembrance that will honor and glorify the Lord, it should be planned with purpose. Each person must be deliberately prayerful, with the Word of God as a guide. The church could assist in helping older adults with this great endeavor! A practical outworking of the theology of aging would call families to care for one another and churches to assist in teaching. Here are some topics to consider:

- *How to be good grandparents*
- *How to honor grandparents and treat them with respect*
- *How to care for adult parents*
- *How to learn to appreciate one another through intergenerational ministries*
- *How to deal with the challenge of missions*
- *How to help seniors find and use their spiritual gifts*

The God of the aging calls the church to support those experiencing various kinds of transitions in family life and to assist in care giving and encouraging spiritual growth.

As with David and Job, the desire would be that the second half of life would be filled with purpose, and lead to a life that would finish well; one that had served the Lord with eternal significance. According to the book of Job, he must have fulfilled God's full purpose with the description of his death: "Job lived on another 140 years, living to see his children and grandchildren—four generations of them! Then he died—an old man, a full life" (Job 42:17, The Message). Look at the end of David's life because it says that he had served his generation by the will of God; his work was finished! "For David, after he had served his own generation by the will of God, fell asleep, was buried with his fathers…" (Acts 13:36).

Let me close this chapter with a story about a man named Lou Forbes, from New Sweden, Maine. Lou was a potato farmer who was forced into early retirement due to bad health. Millie, his wife, continued to work as a school nurse, but used her vacation time to accompany Lou on short-term mission trips that took them to Vietnam, Haiti, and other locations in the USA. I met Lou on a mission trip to Haiti. I learned that he should have died five years prior to that trip because he had such a bad heart condition. What was he doing traveling to foreign lands to do missions when he was

in such bad shape? The doctor said, "Go, but pace yourself! Don't over-do!"

In November of 2003, Lou and Millie were in Arkansas doing a short-term mission project–helping to build a shed. On one of the days when the group broke for lunch, they celebrated Lou's 70th birthday, which happened to be that very day. They went back to work and soon after Lou dropped dead! What a shock to his poor wife, but here was a man who wanted to use his days serving the Lord, and did so up to his last breath. Yes, he was a retired potato farmer who loved the Lord and was faithful in making himself available to God, as long as God gave him life. *Finishing well!* Living with purpose and being prepared for death, as Lou was, up to the very last breath.

What's the Title of *Your* Story?

What will the title of the book that contains your life message proclaim? Each person's book will contain a different story, but the "thread of sameness" in each believer's book should show a life that was faithfully serving God. In the New Testament, we find "God's Hall of Faith" in Hebrews 11. It contains the examples of those whose life message is recorded as an encouragement for others down through the centuries. They are included in that "so great a cloud of witnesses" in heaven that ought to encourage us to *run with endurance the race that is set before us* until God calls us to cross that *bridge of eternal significance.* I hope to hear these words when I cross that finish line: "Well done, good and faithful servant...enter into the joy of thy lord." Will those you lead be added to the list of "faith heroes?" [35]

The following poem by Paul Gilbert is intended to encourage the reader to live life in faithful service so that others will read a life

message that challenges and encourages them to press on toward the mark of the high calling of God.

You're writing a "gospel,"
A chapter each day,
By the deeds that you do,
By the words that you say;
Men read what you write,
Whether faithful or true;
Say, what is the "gospel"
According to you?

From the cassette jacket of Steve Green's *Find Us Faithful* are the following words of introduction to the title song: [36]

Ask faith to look through the keyhole of the promise and tell you what it sees there laid up for him that overcomes: ask it to listen and tell you whether it cannot hear the shout of those crowned saints receiving the reward of all their services and sufferings here on earth. And do you stand on the other side afraid to wet your foot with those sufferings and temptations, which, like a little trickle of water, run between you and glory? [37]

Then follow the words of this great song—reminding the older Christian of the call to faithfulness, with a challenge for each older adult to finish well, leaving behind a wonderful "life message" to be read by all those who come behind them.

"We're pilgrims on the journey
of the narrow road
And those who've gone before us line the way
Cheering on the faithful, encouraging the weary
Their lives a stirring testament to God's sustaining grace.

Surrounded by so great a cloud of witnesses
Let us run the race not only for the prize
But as those who've gone before us
Let us leave to those behind us
The heritage of faithfulness passed on through godly lives.

After all our hopes and dreams have come and gone
And our children sift through all we've left behind
May the clues that they discover and the memories they uncover
Become the light that leads them to the road we each must find.

Oh may all who come behind us find us faithful
May the fire of our devotion light their way
May the footprints that we leave
Lead them to believe
And the lives we live inspire them to obey
Oh may all who come behind us find us faithful." [38]

Reflect and Grow

- *If you are currently over fifty-five, what kind of an adventure are you experiencing? (Be creative! Is it a white-knuckle thrill ride? A steamy romance novel story? A Doctor Doolittle zoo? Etc.) If you are younger, what kind of an adventure would you like to have in the future?*
- *What are your priorities in life? How have they changed in the past twenty years?*
- *Explain this phrase: finish well. Share some steps that you need take in order to reach your goal.*
- *How can you reconnect with God? Give specific examples!*

Chapter Six

The Church Must "Come of Age"

I was leaving the skilled care facility, late one afternoon, and preparing to go home when I saw Jack in the lobby; a resident who had come from my hometown. I said, "Goodnight, Jack, see you tomorrow!" He stopped, pointed his finger at me and said, "Don't say that! Rather say, if the Lord wills, I will see you tomorrow!" Much in Scripture speaks of the "fast" passing of life. James 4:13-15 reads: "Come now, you who say, 'today or tomorrow we will go to such and such a city, spend a year there, buy and sell, and make a profit; whereas you do not know what will happen tomorrow. For what is your life? It is even a vapor that appears for a little time and then vanishes away. Instead you ought to say, 'If the Lord wills, we shall live and do this or that.'"

The Psalmist writes, "Lord make me to know my end, And what is the measure of my days, *that* I may know how frail I *am*. Indeed, You have made my days *as* handbreadths, and my age is as nothing before You; certainly every man at his best state is but vapor. *Selah* Surely every man walks about like a shadow; Surely they busy themselves in vain; He heaps up *riches,* and does not know who will gather them" (Psalm 39:4-6).

Here is another call to live every day with purpose, for none of us knows how long we have upon this earth. Age is as nothing to God! While we have life, we are to live for the glory of God, serving Him, and at peace with Him, so that when our last day is scheduled, we are ready to cross *the bridge of eternal significance,* on our way to heaven. Lamentations 3:22 reminds us "It is of the Lord's mercies that we are not consumed." This says that it is only by God's mercy that we are alive. Life and breath are not deserved; each day that God gives us is precious and a gift from Him. If that is true, then man's life ought to be lived as a gift to Him; "applying our hearts to wisdom" (Psalm 90:10) and "redeeming the time" (Ephesians 5:15-16).

How then shall we live? God says, "For I have created him for my glory" (Isaiah 43:7). As long as we have life we are called to glorify God. What exactly does that mean? In Ephesians 1:12, Paul writes, "We should be to the praise of his glory."

Colonel Rick Husband and six other astronauts were killed on February 1, 2003 when the space shuttle Columbia broke apart minutes after its scheduled launch in Florida. Christian recording artist Steve Green met Husband at a concert a few years before, after which they became friends. In an interview with CNN, Green said, "Rick was a man of faith. He lived with the Christian hope of a better place, a place called heaven. But he also had a fond affection for this place, for this world. And that was his zeal, to spend his life making a difference."[39]

What can a person do to make a difference as he reaches the second half of life? The church needs to challenge baby boomers to start thinking about *what they will do when they grow up,* as they begin to have more discretionary time and funds. Steve Sloan, the editor of AARP's *The Magazine,* and Ken Dychtwald, president

and CEO of Age Wave, a consulting company in San Francisco that specializes in marketing to older consumers, are quoted in *The New York Times* regarding the challenge of getting people of this self-serving generation to volunteer.

Sloan says, "The assumption that they'll be willing to open up their lives after they retire to volunteering may not be true because the people who do it find time for it when they're working. But asking people to volunteer at any time is a good idea."

Dychtwald says, "even if as many as half the retiring baby boomers decide that this is my time and I don't care about anybody else, that would still leave tens of millions of boomers who will decide that's enormously unsatisfying and they would not feel useful if they weren't taking meaningful portions of time to give back. One factor that might make them willing to consider volunteering is that they will be hit by dual liberations, equally potent, leaving them with free time not just for years but for decades: a liberation from full-time work and a liberation from parenting." [40] As these boomers begin to free themselves up as "empty-nesters" and gain more discretionary time and funds, they can begin to make a difference in their church, community, and world. Not all will be interested in short-term missionary travels but for those who are, it gives an opportunity for travel to a foreign country, as well as a purposeful experience of using their gifts and abilities for eternal significance.

The Finisher's Project, now MissionNext, is a great resource for helping boomers find and use their spiritual and natural gifts in missionary endeavors. I mentioned this agency earlier without explanation. This is a mission agency founded by a visionary named Nelson Malwitz. The ministry conducts Finisher's Forums, described by Nelson as an "Urbana for Boomers" in different

locations around the country. In those meetings they seek to interest and challenge those in the second half of life to consider short-term missions, or perhaps a change of career to a full-time mission experience. They have a recruiting department where they match gifts and abilities of those who submit a form by computer to the needs of mission-sending organizations. In March 1998 the Finishers Project published a survey of 600 people from the American baby boom generation (age 42-55) that reported the thinking of this age group regarding retirement—it's timing and activities. Early in the survey a question was asked, "How many years before you are planning to retire?" The average was thirteen years. After questions regarding ministry and missions were asked, the response to the question, "How many years before they *could* retire" was reduced to six years."[41] Properly challenged and with training, there are perhaps a fair number of boomers ready to accept the challenge of missions—short-term or career. What a wonderful thing—to help those fifty years plus adults take the successes and lessons learned in the first half of life and turn them into significance in the second half.

Outreach and Interesting Ideas for Boomers

Outreach to Boomers, who are friends of church members or attendees, might be accomplished through well-planned, non-threatening, first class activities. A suggestion that came out of a training conference for older adult ministries was to plan a dinner cruise on a harbor of the ocean, or a lake, with a gospel jazz band doing music. The spiritual input for the evening would be just a simple prayer for the meal, a short devotional or testimony, and a closing prayer. The idea would be to keep the evening "low-key" spiritually, and build relationships that would open up more opportunities to share Christ in the future. Other areas of interest

where the church might serve as a resource for boomers are: caring for older adult parents, financial planning for retirement, medical concerns, housing options, answering the *questions: What can I do now that I've grown up; or, How can I develop meaningful experiences for serving the Lord?*

As people reach the second half of life, they can be categorized in many ways. Some have referred to the young-old (50-65 years), middle-old (66-80 years), and the old-old (80+ years). Another way to look at it is in Life Stages describing with the same age brackets as: Mid-Life, Retired Life, and Senior Life. A light-hearted description might be the "go-go's, the slow-go's, and the no-go's." I have come across some other terms used to describe aging as creative, productive, transformed, conscious, and/or successful. In the coming years, aging will continue to be redefined by sociologists, researchers, and the demographics. The church will have to program and reach out with specialized and intentional programming and groups. It would probably be wise for evangelical seminaries to include some courses in understanding and meeting the needs of adults in the second half of life.

As a person "grows up" into those older adult years, is there still life in the church? The question I asked in an article that I wrote years ago is still relevant: *Where is the Church When the Hair Turns Gray.*[42] Another article, *"Too Old? Never!"*[43] a few years later, highlighted surprising ministry opportunities that the residents of the retirement community that I served as Chaplain were accomplishing. As long as a person has life, he is called to glorify God and serve Him.

Camp Grandma and Grandpa

Let me review some of the interesting and creative ministries in which the residents of the retirement community I served were

involved. Two of the residents as camp grandma and grandpa at at a denomination camp one summer. Their responsibilities were few, but important. They were to be there, be available, be a friend to the junior campers; many who were away from home for the very first time.

Go-to Grandma and Grandpa

Another summer the residents teamed up with Child Evangelism Fellowship of Connecticut to conduct a five-day club for neighborhood children in kindergarten through grade 6. The children knew that they could go to these folks with questions, boo-boo's, for hugs etc. They helped with crafts, baked cookies, passed out invitations in the neighborhood, took attendance, participated in the daily meetings, and were involved in checking the follow-up studies. Some could not do a whole lot, but they were prayer partners. The greatest joy came from knowing that three children put their trust in Christ.

More Than a Bible Study Is the Heart Study

One girl remains a friend of my daughter and continues her walk in the Lord because a group of elderly residents in an *old folk's home* decided to reach their neighborhood for Christ. This wasn't the first time! When I first came to Elim Park, a group of ladies led a Bible study, on the porch of one of their homes. Four high school girls in the neighborhood came weekly to have a Bible study, do crafts, and enjoy some refreshments prepared by the residents. It was not just the Bible study that caught their attention; it was how these women opened their hearts to the younger girls. Again, one of those young ladies accepted the Lord, and today continues her walk with the Lord and is married to a pastor.

If you have a retirement home in your community, or active senior adults in your church, what creative ways can you use to reach out to young people? Maybe some could serve as a grandma or grandpa for the Sunday school, the vacation Bible school or boys and girls clubs? Two of our residents at age eighty and ninety years old used to go to a nearby church, every week, to listen to Pioneer Clubbers recite their memory work. Another resident who moved away from our retirement community enjoyed being called "Grandpa Russ," as he visited his church nursery school two to three times a week, and shared some of his life stories and experiences with the children. Some of those children did not have grandparents living close by and adopted this man to serve in that position.

If you have a nursery school, or Sunday school, you could start a secret prayer partner program between the generations, or have some of the older adults read to the children. One church I visited utilizes the retired men to serve in the "fix-it crew" (Nehemiah's Helpers) one day a week to accomplish those little repairs (and some major ones too) that the regular maintenance crew has on a continuing "to do" list.

Here are some great ways that seniors can get involved in the church. These all came from actual real-life situations or are suggested by the author.

❖ *One man came to his pastor the week after his retirement and said, "Pastor, I am retired now. I'll give one day a week to do whatever you would like me to do." He assisted in visitation and other tasks that were helpful to that pastor.*

❖ *Another man who was retired as an executive of a large company became "church administrator" one day a week.*

❖ *A number of years ago, a seventy-year old couple that had*

retired a few years earlier, came to their pastor and the husband said, "I was a company executive and have a financial background, and my wife was a secretary. What can we do for the church?" There was a need for secretarial help in the church office that the wife fulfilled on a part-time basis, and they both became involved in the pastor's pre-marital counseling session on budgeting.

❖ Perhaps visiting the shut-ins and recording their testimonies of God's faithfulness through the years, or how they came to trust Jesus Christ as Savior would be a blessing to the church body. The recorded message could then be shared in a Sunday school class or church service, and still keep the person "connected."

❖ The person could even share some prayer requests for which the church could pray.

❖ Older adults make great greeters on Sunday, daily telephone reassurance ministers, greeting card ministers, or can run errands for others in need.

❖ One elderly lady took it upon herself to send a bulletin to all those regular attendees and members that were absent on a given Sunday. She did that on Sunday afternoon, so that it would be in the mailbox on Tuesday of those who missed the service.

❖ In some churches the older adults keep the tract racks, pew racks, or other publication racks up to date.

❖ Another church has a monthly outreach luncheon for the older adults of their church. The church members are encouraged to invite friends in the community to come, and each month they host seventy to eighty seniors; about two-thirds of them are from outside the church.

There are many ways for those who are retired to remain active in ministry. What can you add to this list?

Falling Through the Cracks is Painful

Don't let them become *spiritually senile,* by allowing them to simply live in or remember only the past. I used to receive a newsletter for the older adults of a church in Minnesota and my favorite column was called

> Don't let them become *spiritually senile,* by allowing them to simply live in or remember only the past.

The Stewardship Report where it listed the time commitments and ministry jobs accomplished by the seniors in the church. It was a nice reminder that they are still useful and valued in the total ministry of a local church. Let me try to relate a story that I heard at a seminar a number of years ago. It illustrates how even a home-bound member could be valued and involved in serving the local church and leadership even though she was unable to attend church on a regular basis.

The pastor made a visit to the home of a woman who had not been able to be in church for some time. She indicated that she wished she could still help somehow. The pastor said that he had a mailing that he wished to send to the membership, and could use some help stuffing the envelopes. She said that she would love to assist with that project but she would not be able to do it as quickly as he might want it done. He said that it would be helpful no matter how long it took and brought the mailing to her the next day. A number of days passed and he did not hear from her, so he phoned, and she said that she had just a few more to do if he wished to pick them up later in the day.

When he arrived, she was still finishing up the last couple, and he watched as she slowly folded the last few letters and with some difficulty stuffed them into the envelopes. She said, "Now you see why it took me so long!" And then proceeded to tell her pastor that not only did she have some difficulty getting each letter into the envelope, but also when the envelope was complete, she then held each letter up before the Lord and prayed specifically for the person or the family. This pastor had a deacon's committee meeting that night and shared with the men that he had learned that day the source of any success that the church was having. He told them that he had learned about a *powerhouse for prayer* that was fueling any growth of the church and change in people's lives.

> **We might be considered "junk" in our sinful selves, but God loves to take our junk and put His value upon it and with age we become more like an antique of great value.**

The church is growing older and it must come of age! Are your church and your attitude hospitable toward the older adults in your church? Do you really want them involved? Are you interested in helping them *finish well?*

I was at a restaurant recently when a sign on the wall caught my attention. It read, "We buy junk and sell antiques. We might be considered "junk" in our sinful state, but God loves to take our junk and put His value upon it; with age we become more like an antique of great value.

We know that age only increases the value of an antique. God, the owner/designer of this treasure, sent his Son to redeem this precious, created possession. As it is brought back to the antique

store (heaven), the Owner of this greatly valued treasure is glad to have in His presence that which has *eternal* value.

Let's remember that the human treasure, which was made in God's image, has had value all along. Isaiah 43:1, describing the Redeemer of Israel as knowing each piece and it's whereabouts throughout life's journey. "But now, thus says the LORD, who created you... And He who formed you: 'Fear not, for I have redeemed you; I have called you by your name; You are Mine.'" As an antique gets older, and the value of age is recognized, it becomes a treasure. It must be carefully cared for and protected because it has a history that is shared with family and friends. The Designer/Creator wants to be involved in the life of that treasure according to Isaiah 46:4 which reads, "Even to your old age, I am He, And even to gray hairs I will carry you! I have made, and I will bear; Even I will carry, and will deliver you." God's design seems to be that the church family and biological family should take responsibility to carry out that verse. Our seniors are a treasure, created to be respected, and always connected to the believing community and the family with whom God chose to place them.

Ethel Waters, the actress and renowned singer with the Billy Graham crusades, was often heard to say, "I know I'm somebody: 'Cause God don't make no junk.'" [44] Born as a result of the rape of her mother at age twelve and raised in poverty, she was able to testify after her new birth in Jesus, that regardless of the situation, God never makes junk! And she seemed to finish the race having served the Lord and bringing a blessing to many who heard her testimony and her song.

May you, the reader; a seminarian, church pastor, counselor, teacher, community leader, family member or whoever God brought to the pages of this book, bring a blessing to and through

the lives of the older adults that God has entrusted to your care. Help them finish well! Let them finish as a treasure and not a forgotten curbside piece of trash waiting for the next pick up. May what you do with the challenges found in this book bring glory to God.

Reflect and Grow

- *How do we move our thinking about seniors from trash to treasures?*
- *What is one way that you can bless a senior today?*
- *If you are a senior, how can you be a blessing in your family, church and community?*

Endnotes

1. A ministry of Converge Worldwide (aka: the Baptist General Conference) www.convergeww.org : and the Converge Northeast (aka: Northeast Baptist Conference) www.convergenortheast.org.

2. Glenn B. Havumaki, "A Hidden People in Plain View," Posted: 3/29/11 online at: www.convergeworldwide.org/news/hidden-people-plain-view

3. From Meet Yourself in the Psalms by Warren Wiersbe, Copyright ©1983 quoted online: http://www.2prophetu.com/templates/!print/details.asp?id=35585&PG=resources&CID=17783

4. Charles G. Oakes, *Working the Gray Zone* (Franklin, TN, Providence House Publishers, 2000), 15.

5. Michael Vitez, "A Generation Takes Up Autobiography," Reprinted by permission from *The Philadelphia Inquirer,* February 20, 2000 in *Agenda,* Number 92 (July, 2000), pp. 2-3.

6. Paul Lee Tan. *Encyclopedia of 7,700 Illustrations: Signs of the Times* (Rockville, MD: Assurance Publishers, 1979), 772-773: #'s 3264 – 3269 and 3271.

7. *Working in the Gray Zone*, p. 46.

8. In the Old Testament, the widows were to be cared for by the Levites from the tithes that the people gave to support the priesthood: "And the Levite, because he has no portion nor inheritance with you, and the stranger and the fatherless *and the widows who are within your gates, may come and eat and be satisfied, that the LORD your God may bless you* in all the work of your hand which you do" (Deuteronomy 14:29). Again, the caring for widows reflects our relationship to God and brings God's blessing upon his servants.

9. *Working in the Gray Zone.* pp. 7-8.

10. Thorson, James A. and Thomas C. Cook, ed., *Spiritual Well-Being of the Elderly* (Springfield, IL: Charles C. Thomas Publishers) 1980, pp. 38-50.

11. *The Value of Age*, Don Norbie, Milk and Honey, November, 1992: A non-profit ministry of Spread the Word, Inc., 2721 Oberlin Drive, York, PA. 17404.

12. "Older Christians are Leaving Churches" by Wayne J. Edwards, *Pulpit Helps,* March, 2006. The article was adapted from the book, Raising the Standard, by Wayne J. Edwards.

13. From a paper by David C. Davis, *A Pastoral Ministry to Older Persons.* A copy of this paper was given to me by my pastor

who had attended a seminar from which he received the notes. It does not give any further information but the notes were quite helpful.

14. In a paper titled "Grief and Loss in the Aging Process" by Timothy J. Wildman, D. Min., which was produced for the Gerontology Forum (Boston 1983), there is a reference to an article *Loss, Depletion and Restitution* in the book *Geriatric Psychology* (International Universities Press 1962).

15. Nona Smith, 1978. Nona was a college student at Barrington College, Barrington, RI and to my knowledge never copyrighted or recorded her song. I received it from the gerontology professor at the time.

16. James J. Farrell. "Botox" in the *Clergy Journal* Volume LXXXI, Number 2, November/December, 2004.

17. "The Future Is Now" in the *Record-Journal*, Meriden, CT., Wednesday, January 17, 2007, p. 5.

18. Charles Arn, *White Unto Harvest* Monrovia, CA: Institute for American Church Growth, 2003, p. 18.

19. David C. Baker, "Spiritual Care for the New Millenium," *Provider*, January, 2000, p. 51.

20. Bob Buford, *Halftime* (Grand Rapids: Zondervan Publishing House, 1994), p. 15.

21. Vision New England 50+ Age Wave Conference in Lexington, MA, April 2002.

22. Paul Tournier, *The Adventure of Living*, San Francisco: HarperCollins , June 1979), pp. 236ff.

23. Dr. Henry M. Morris, World Publishing, Inc, Grand Rapids, 1995, p. 1032.

24. "The Soul-making Years," AGEnda, Number 97, October 2001.

25. (Psalm 107:35 KJV) "He turneth the wilderness into a standing water, and dry ground into watersprings…And sow the fields, and plant vineyards, which may yield fruits of increase."

26. W. Glyn Evans, *Daily with the King*, Chicago: Moody Bible Institute, 1979, January 25, p. 25.

27 Ibid, 1318.

28. Ibid, 228.

29. Ibid, 22.

30. Ibid, 231.

31. Ibid, 24

32. John R. Cross. *The Stranger on the Road to Emmaus, 3rd Edition.* (Canada: Goodseed International, 1997), p. 10.

33. Consider writing a legacy letter: www.legacyletter.org

34. Sunday School lessons produced by Grady R. Henley and made available by email, periodically, to those on his mailing list. This particular one was received on November 12, 2000.

35. Hebrews 12:1 and Matthew 25:21.

36. Copyright © 1987 Birdwing Music (ASCAP) (adm. at EMICMGPublishing.com)/Jonathan Mark Music (ASCAP). All rights reserved. Used by permission.

37. William Gurnall, "The Christian in Complete Armor," published by Banner of Truth.

38. Find Us Faithful. Words and Music by Jon Mohr. Copyright © 1987 Jonathan Mark Music, Birdwing Music. All rights reserved. Used by permission.

39. Kirsten Burke, "A Triumph in Tragedy," *Power for Living* (Volume 63, Number 2), 3.

40. Stuart Elliot, "Persuading Retiring Baby Boomers to Volunteer," *The New York Times,* January 6, 2005. http://www.agewave.com/media_files/nyt2.html.

41. The full report and information about the Finishers Project can be obtained by contacting the organization: P.O. Box 12649, Chandler, AZ 85428-0028. Phone (484) 584-5448 http://www.finishers.org

42. Glenn B. Havumaki, "Where Is the Church When the Hair Turns Gray?" *The Standard,* Volume 69, Number 7, July/August, 1979, 31.

43. Glenn B. Havumaki, "Too Old? Never!" *The Standard,* Volume 75, Number 5, May 1985, 46-47.

44. Harold Herring. "I Am Somebody Because God Don't Make No Junk," http://www.debtfreearmy.org/rich-thoughts-blogs/900-i-am-somebody-because-god-dont-make-no-junk, (Accessed on March 22, 2012).

LINKS AND MINISTRIES MENTIONED IN THE BOOK

Christ Above Politics, https://christabovepolitics.com
PO Box 11 Drasco, AR 72530 Telephone: (888) 474-4727/
admin@ChristAbovePolitics.com

Christian Grandparenting Network christiangrandparenting.com
Sherry Schumann, President sschumann@christiangrandparenting.com

Community Chaplain Service Executive Director Rev. William H. Echols PO Box 117 Foxboro, MA 02035 Email: commchap74@gmail.com Telephone 508-505-0787 A ministry to train volunteer chaplains to minister to the spiritual needs of residents in Care Centers.

Elder Care and Links, Dr. Tom McCormick Email: twmc.gta@gmail.com A periodic email of many resources from Tom who is a tremendous researcher, author, and Nursing Home Chaplain

ElderQuest: Engaging the Generations Cavin T. Harper, Executive Director/Author/Speaker www.elderquestmin.com Seminar Presenter: Courageous Grandparenting Seminars; Family Discipleship Conferences; Inter-generational Discipling; Grandparents Raising Grandchildren; Rachel Project Books: Courageous Grandparenting; Grandparents raising grandchildren, Others found on website. Contact: cavin@cavinharper.com; Telephone 719-552-1404

Elim Park Baptist Home, Inc. www.elimpark.org A Continuing Care Retirement Community located in central Connecticut with 500 residents and 350+ staff. Telephone: 203-272-3547

Evangelical Covenant Church of America
SENIOR ADULT MINISTRY: CRESCENDO.
https://covchurch.org/make-and-deepen-disciples/crescendo/
Contact: Evelyn Johnson - emrj217@gmail.com

God Cares Ministry, Bill Goodrich President & Founder, Has incorporated SonShine Ministry. Ministry of Training and Equipping God's people to help nursing home residents find hope and peace in Jesus. Watch Introductory Video Here Helpful Resources in large print hymn books, videos, and other useful materials Nursing Home ministry. Contact: https://www.godcaresministry.com/ Telephone: 440-930-9173

GRANDS N' CHARGE. Gloria Williams, Founder and President. Springfield, MA. Gloria is empowering Grandparents to understand their rights and what they are entitled to receive while their grandchild/ren are in their care. Contact: https://www.grandparentsncharge.com/ Telephone: 413-788-0234

MissionNext (formerly The Finisher's) missionnext.org
Whether you are looking to serve part-time or full-time, short-term or long-term, you will find multiple positions available with global mission agencies and Christian Schools that fit your skills, experience, and ministry preferences. Complete just one profile and allow our unique matching system to provide you with a list of jobs, mission agencies, and schools that would be an ideal fit. Contact those that are greatest interest to you.

Spiritual Eldercare: Founder, Chaplain Elisa Bosley in Boulder, CO Ministering to Older Adults with Alzheimer's Disease and other Dementias. Does a great planning worship services for care centers, and always plans specifically for special day services. Contact: https://spiritualeldercare.com

Senior Adult Ministries: Assemblies of God (USA) https://sam.ag.org/ Dr. G. Robert (Bob) Cook, Jr. and his wife, Sherilyn, serve as the leaders of the Senior Adult Ministries department of the Assemblies of God. Contact by email: bobcook@ag.org Download the current issue of Primeline: Spring 2023 Issue (PDF).

Senior Living Ministries Devotional Dr. Michael Risley, Executive Director. You can request a daily (M-F) email copy by signing up at: Request the Daily Living Devotional online at https://www.seniorlivingministries.org/#devotional-signup

Significant Living Travel, Tours geared for Christian older adults Founded by Christina and Andrew Knowles. Contact: https://significantlivingtravel.com/ Telephone: 760-515-6083

The OLDst MINISTRY PARADIGM
https://paradigm2.org/ books/ Celebrating Ministry To and with Older Adults. Here is a listing of books still in or out of print. A good resource on many different subjects for this ministry

THE UPPER ROOM OLDER ADULT MINISTRY

https://www.google.com/search?q=the+upper+room+old-eradult+ministry&rlz=1C1GCEU_enUS883US909&o-=The+Upper+Room&aqs=chrome.2.0i131i433i512j69i-64j69i59j0i512j0i131i433i512j69i60l3.24146j1j7&sourceid=chrome&ie=UTF-8

www.ingramcontent.com/pod-product-compliance
Lightning Source LLC
Chambersburg PA
CBHW051209120626
46547CB00013B/1271